Praise for *How to Age Joyfully*

"This is an outstanding book. It carries a clear message and expresses a clear philosophy, namely that we need to transform the way we think about living longer. Science has now made clear that even though there is a process called ageing, a normal biological process which does have some effects, these effects are relatively insignificant until the late nineties. Most of the problems people face are preventable and remediable, and the book not only explains this but gives advice, insight and encouragement. It speaks from the heart, from an author who has knowledge and experience. It is a manifesto for living better longer."
Sir Muir Gray, CBE, FRCPSGlas, FCLIP, Professor and Consultant in Public Health, Oxford University; author of *Sod 70!*; first Chief Knowledge Officer for the NHS and creator of NHS Choices

"We are all ageing. This motivating and practical book is a valuable, easy-to-read guide on what we need to do to help us age well and make the most of our lives. As a patron of Open Age, I'm delighted that a share of Maggy's royalties will benefit this remarkable charity."
Baroness Sally Greengross, Chief Executive, International Longevity Centre UK; member of the House of Lords since 2000 and co-chair of several All-Party Parliamentary Groups on ageing; Director General of Age Concern England from 1987–2000

"As a society, we should be celebrating the extraordinary gift of longer life that we have been given by the last century's advances in public health, nutrition and medicine. But instead, our ageing population is all too often presented as a problem rather than a gift, and ageist stereotypes and age discrimination are everywhere – in our media, our workplaces, our towns, and in our own worries and attitudes about growing old. How to Age Joyfully *is a welcome antidote to this fearful, negative view of ageing, and a rich resource of ideas and evidence for how to enjoy your own later life."*
Catherine Foot, Director of Evidence, Centre for Ageing Better

"We hear so much about the burdens of an ageing society that we seem to have talked ourselves into thinking of rising life expectancy as a bad thing. In this book, Maggy Pigott reminds us how lucky we are to live at such a time and how to add joy to all the other emotions as we navigate those later years."
Alan Johnson, former Labour politician and Cabinet Minister, including Secretary of State for Health (2007–2009); award-winning author; patron of Open Age

"Full of wit, wisdom – and hope!"
Gyles Brandreth, writer and broadcaster

"We all know that people today can expect to live healthily and productively for longer than ever before. This is fact. Irrefutable. But, what is less clear is what we are all to do with this extra time. As the concept of retirement is increasingly eroded, our society is in desperate need of new life models, new examples of what is possible. We need new champions to help shape a new world, where people can work, play, innovate, inspire, lead and create – throughout life, regardless of age. Maggy is such a champion. Read her book and see why."
Dr Jonathan Collie, co-founder of The Age of No Retirement

"A fun and savvy guide to putting more life in your years."
Carl Honoré, writer and broadcaster; author of *In Praise of Slow* (2004) and *Bolder: Making the Most of our Longer Lives* (2018).

"Old age is being redefined and this is an essential book for today's new world. It is full of positive actions to maximise enjoyment of our added years in this amazing period of life."
Joyce Williams MBE FCSP, aka blogger GrandmaWilliams.com

HOW TO AGE JOYFULLY

Copyright © Maggy Pigott, 2019

All rights reserved.

An Hachette UK Company
www.hachette.co.uk

Vie Books, an imprint of Summersdale Publishers Ltd
Part of Octopus Publishing Group Limited
Carmelite House
50 Victoria Embankment
LONDON
EC4Y 0DZ
UK

www.summersdale.com

Printed and bound in the Czech Republic

ISBN: 978-1-78685-968-6

Substantial discounts on bulk quantities of Summersdale books are available to corporations, professional associations and other organizations. For details contact general enquiries: telephone: +44 (0) 1243 771107 or email: enquiries@summersdale.com.

Note: The advice in this book is written to the best of the author's knowledge and research but should not be used as a substitute for medical advice. Please consult professional help where necessary.

"I commend this book to everyone of all ages, and let us all age joyfully!" **Dame Judi Dench**

HOW TO AGE
JOYFULLY

Eight Steps to a Happier, Fuller Life

MAGGY PIGOTT
FOREWORD BY DAME JUDI DENCH

THE FUTURE DEPENDS ON WHAT YOU DO TODAY.

Mahatma Gandhi

How To Age Joyfully is dedicated to my husband, Tim, and children, Mike and Rachel, who do so much to help me age joyfully.

I am grateful to my family and friends for their help, suggestions and belief in the book's potential – and their promises to buy several copies each, if published!

Thanks also go to the inspirational charity Open Age, an exemplar of much of what is contained in this guide. I am donating 50 per cent of my royalties after tax to Open Age, which does so much to help the over fifties enjoy active and fulfilling lives. (Open Age is registered as a charity in England and Wales No:1160125. www.openage.org.uk).

I am extremely grateful to Catherine Foot, Director of Evidence at the Centre for Ageing Better, for her very positive and helpful feedback on reading the manuscript.

And finally, huge thanks to all at Summersdale for their skill and guidance, in particular, Claire Plimmer, Editorial Director, for taking a chance on a novice author and Claire Berrisford, my editor, for her unwavering enthusiasm, support and patience.

YOU ONLY LIVE ONCE, BUT IF YOU DO IT RIGHT, ONCE IS ENOUGH.

Mae West

CONTENTS

FOREWORD

This is a book that I believe is long overdue, and I was delighted when Maggy Pigott asked me to write the foreword.

Anyone who knows me – and quite a few who do not – are aware that the word "Retire" is not mentioned in my house. These days, we are all living longer, and we should make the most of our extra years. That includes keeping on working if that is what you want to do. If that is not your choice, there are lots of ways to keep active and to enjoy older age. This book tells you about some of them.

Open Age is a charity which will benefit from the sales of this book. Based in London, it provides a wide range of physical, creative and mentally stimulating activities to enable older people to make new friends, while developing new skills, and learning to fulfil their potential.

I commend this book to everyone of all ages, and let us all *age joyfully!*

Dame Judi Dench, April 2019

WE'RE LIVING LONGER — LET'S LIVE BETTER!

Let us cherish and love old age; for it is full of pleasure, if one knows how to use it.

Seneca (4 BCE–CE 65, Roman Stoic philosopher and statesman)

Thanks to science, better health care, healthier lifestyles and higher living standards we are faced with the global phenomenon of an ageing population. Longevity is increasing in almost every country, although the rate differs depending on economic, social and various other factors. By 2050, about two billion people in the world (one in five of us) will be aged 60 and older. And the numbers of those in their eighties, nineties and even one-hundreds are increasing at the fastest rate.

This longevity should be celebrated and encouraged. Older people can offer so much, including experience, wisdom, skills, work, love, caring, emotional stability, perspective, fun, time and money. Everyone benefits – from the individuals themselves, and their family and friends, to the wider community.

Ageing is not lost youth but a new stage of opportunity and strength.
Betty Friedan (1921–2006, writer and author of
The Fountain of Age, activist and feminist who lived to 85)

But if added years are to be a bonus, not a burden, we need to keep healthy enough to enjoy them. We owe it to ourselves, those close to us and society, to do what we can to make our old age the best it can be – **"the crown of life"** (Marcus Tullius Cicero, 106–43 BCE, Roman philosopher, politician, lawyer). I hope this book will help you to achieve that.

If I'd known how old I was going to be I'd have taken better care of myself.
Adolph Zuckor (1873–1976, film producer and
founder of Paramount Pictures, lived to 103)

MY STORY

**There is no old age. There is,
as there always was, just you.**
Carol Matthau (1924–2003, actress and author)

I'm fast approaching 70 chronologically but, inside, I've not changed. I'm still me, and that "me" feels young. I don't see myself as the "oldie" I appear to be to those who kindly offer me their seat on the bus.

At 59 I retired from a public service desk job, due to ill health. With no plans and no idea what the future might hold, I was worried that the best part of my life was over, even when my health and energy began to improve.

To dance is to live.
Charles M. Schulz (1922–2000,
cartoonist and creator of *Peanuts*)

I'd never danced, apart from at parties and an unsuccessful attempt at ballet at nursery school. But, in my mid-fifties, Latin dance classes at my local gym changed everything. I discovered I adored dancing, despite failing to remember steps or keep in time with the music – usually both. When I braved Argentine tango lessons, I became addicted and practised "ganchos" and "boleos" (hooks, kicks and flicks) in the embrace of any man brave enough (or foolish enough) to dance with me!

In my sixties, with some trepidation, I returned to ballet, this time with a rather more "mature" age group! I was surprised to find I was a youngster, our oldest participant being a youthful 90-plus. Although still lacking talent, I found I now loved ballet.

With perseverance, countless classes, and avoiding mirrors (as reality didn't help), my dancing very gradually improved. I even took part in a performance or two. At 66 years of age, a little miracle happened. I was accepted into a ballet-based performing company for those over 55, run by a former soloist at the Royal Ballet. I was thrilled – my children were incredulous.

> **You don't stop dancing because you grow old,**
> **you grow old because you stop dancing.**
> Anonymous

Dance is now my passion and it's been life-changing. It has improved my physical and mental health and well-being, motivated me to eat better, to get and stay fitter, challenged my body and mind, increased my confidence, and transported me to a totally different world with fabulous new friends.

I know that however much I dance, or for however long, I'll never be as good as most other dancers, but one of the benefits of ageing is that I just don't care. I love what I *can* do, and now, in my late sixties, I tell everyone: *"I'm a dancer."* I have the pink ballet pumps and gold tango shoes (with stiletto heels I can barely walk in, let alone dance in) to prove it!

I plan to keep on dancing and, if I ever need a stick, I'll drench it in glitter and sequins and channel my inner Fred Astaire with his top hat and cane.

He that does good to another does good also to himself.
Seneca (4 BCE–CE 65, Roman Stoic philosopher and statesman)

Encouraged by having achieved something totally outside my comfort zone, I tried a few more new activities, from singing to T'ai Chi, with huge enjoyment but varying degrees of success. The classes were at Open Age, an inspirational charity helping those over 50 to age healthily and happily. After a couple of years, I became a Trustee and then Vice Chair (also new experiences). I'm donating some of the proceeds of this book's sales to Open Age so, by buying it, you'll be helping others age better too. Visit www.openage.org.uk.

I love volunteering and undoubtedly gain far more than I give, acquiring new skills, purpose, fulfilment and being part of a great community. It is also rewarding to give something back, now that I have the time and the freedom to do so.

A few years post-retirement, I realized two things.

First, that I'd become happier and increasingly grateful for my life, family, friends and good (enough) health.

Second, that ageing has had a very bad press – usually portraying older people as burdens on society with frequent photos of wrinkly hands, hunched backs, walking sticks and more. These negative stereotypes bore little, or no, relation to my life or the lives of most of my contemporaries in their sixties and seventies.

I decided to create a Twitter account, *Age Joyfully @AgeingBetter*, to promote a more realistic picture of getting older. My goal was 100 followers, but I'm astonished to find that I now have thousands of followers who want to share the joys and positive aspects of ageing. The number grows weekly – please join them.

> **If there's a book that you want to read, but it hasn't been written yet, then you must write it.**
> Toni Morrison (born 1931, novelist)

My Twitter account's unexpected popularity was the main inspiration for this book, especially when I realized only a comparatively small number of older people use Twitter! I also wanted to find a better way to pass on what I'd learned about ageing from my personal experience, Open Age, Twitter, published research, and from many others far better qualified than me. *How to Age Joyfully* was born – a little book with a big mission.

I must stress that this is not a medical book, although it is based on evidence and research. I am not a doctor and do not possess a qualification in gerontology – or any other "ology"! This project has been a labour of love for a novice writer. I hope you enjoy reading it as much as I've enjoyed producing it, and that you'll find it both a useful guide and an inspirational companion for this exciting chapter of your life.

THE EIGHT STEPS TO AGEING JOYFULLY

**Youthfulness is about how you live,
not when you were born.**
Karl Lagerfeld (1933–2019, fashion designer
and creative director of Chanel)

The World Health Organization defines health as: "a state of complete physical, mental and social well-being." Society, the economy, our genes, our personal and financial circumstances, illness, life events, and other matters beyond our control can all affect how well we age. But, happily, whether or not we have good health is in large measure down to our behaviour, rather than heredity or "fate". Although there are no guarantees, **most of us can make a significant and positive difference to our quality of life**.

IN THE LONG RUN, WE SHAPE
OUR LIVES, AND WE SHAPE
OURSELVES. THE PROCESS
NEVER ENDS UNTIL WE DIE.
AND THE CHOICES WE MAKE
ARE ULTIMATELY OUR
OWN RESPONSIBILITY.

Eleanor Roosevelt
(1884–1962, political figure and activist)

There is no "silver bullet" to ageing well, but in this book I have identified eight ingredients that, according to evidence and research, are key components for a healthy, happy and longer life. They are:

- being physically active,
- eating a healthy, balanced diet,
- having something to live for, a purpose,
- getting, and staying, socially engaged,
- lifelong learning,
- being grateful,
- giving to others, and
- being positive.

Although these eight recommendations are aimed primarily at those in the second half of life, they apply equally well whether you are 19 or 91. It's never too early – as well as never too late – to start.

Old age is like everything else... to make a success of it, you've got to start young.
Theodore Roosevelt (1858–1919, twenty-sixth US president)

And, although this is not a book about financial matters, it is worth mentioning that starting early also applies to thinking about how much money you will need as you age. Financial security obviously contributes to a better later life so planning ahead and, for example, paying into a pension are very important.

THE SECRET TO LIVING WELL AND LONGER IS TO EAT HALF, WALK DOUBLE, LAUGH TRIPLE AND LOVE WITHOUT MEASURE.

Tibetan proverb

WHY BOTHER?

It's not the years in your life but the
life in your years that counts.
Adlai Stevenson II (1900–1965, lawyer, politician and diplomat)

If you follow the eight-point plan in this book you will be taking actions that, according to research, will improve the health of your body and mind whatever your age. You will definitely enjoy your later life a lot more – and you will probably live longer too. You will age *joyfully*!

Luckily many of the eight steps interconnect so doing one will help you to achieve another. And having limited means is no barrier – many are free or at very low cost. **Even if you only follow one or two steps – in whatever order you fancy – you will benefit and feel better.**

Research has found five regions in the world where people live the longest. They are called the Blue Zones and are located in Japan, Costa Rica, Italy, California and Greece. These areas share lifestyle characteristics that contribute to their inhabitants' longevity. These characteristics are, in essence, the first four steps in this book, namely physical activity, a good diet, purpose, and social engagement together with close family ties.

Healthy citizens are the greatest
asset any country can have.
Winston Churchill (1874–1965, UK prime minister and writer)

AGE ISN'T

HOW OLD YOU ARE BUT HOW OLD

YOU FEEL.

Gabriel Garcia Marquez
(1927–2014, novelist who lived to 87)

GROW OLD ALONG WITH ME. THE BEST IS YET TO BE.

Robert Browning (1812–1889, poet)

TIPS

If not now, when?
Hillel the Elder (110 BCE–CE 10, Jewish religious leader)

TIP 1

You are in control of your life. Believe you can improve it. Every day brings opportunities but only you can grasp them and resolve to act.

The first step is you have to say that you can.
Will Smith (born 1968, actor, producer and comedian)

TIP 2

Start today. Don't procrastinate waiting for the "right time" – such as the New Year, after your holiday, when you've lost weight, or when you feel better. No one lives forever and time seems to accelerate with every passing year. The right time is right now.

If we wait for the moment when everything, absolutely everything is ready, we shall never begin.
Ivan Turgenev (1818–1883, writer)

TIP 3

Change one thing for the better, however small, and then build on your success. Take baby steps. Find what works for you and what you enjoy.

> **A journey of a thousand miles begins with a single step.**
> Lao-Tzu (Sixth century BCE, Chinese philosopher and writer)

TIP 4

Be patient and kind to yourself. There are a great many different suggestions in this small book. If you try to do too much, too fast, you may be setting yourself up to fail, and so give up altogether. Don't be over-ambitious or unrealistic – then, once you start, you may surprise yourself.

> **Start by doing what's necessary; then what's possible;**
> **and suddenly you're doing the impossible.**
> Saint Francis of Assisi (1181–1226, friar)

TIP 5

Persevere, and don't give up. Celebrate success. Celebrate every achievement but equally, if you fail, try again.

> **It does not matter how slowly you go**
> **as long as you do not stop.**
> Confucius (551–479 BCE, Chinese philosopher,
> teacher and politician)

THE STEPS

The golden age is before us.
William Shakespeare (1564 baptized–1616,
playwright, poet and actor)

STEP 1: MOVE

This step is not about moving to a rose-covered country cottage but about being **physically active**.

In 2018 the World Health Organization reported wide-ranging research showing that more than one in four adults globally (28 per cent or 1.4 billion people) are physically inactive. Earlier generations were more active at work and at home and also when at leisure. Now we lead more sedentary lives. Many spend up to 12 hours a day sitting.

Various factors are to blame, including urbanization, better transport and ever-improving technology. Life has been made "easier" for us and a whole raft of daily physical activities have diminished or disappeared. For example, more of us are driving to a large supermarket, or shopping and accessing services online, instead of walking to our local shops or the bank. Even tiny changes can all add up. We watch films on our smart televisions or devices, we don't even have to get up from the sofa to change the television channel, and we can have "takeaways" delivered to our door. These, and many other changes, result in our not moving regularly enough and frequently enough throughout the day.

The result? Physical inactivity is now a serious global health problem. And, unfortunately, as people get older, they become even less active.

In addition to these external factors, there's a long list of reasons individuals give for *inactivity* including:

- not knowing where to take exercise,

- facilities being unavailable,

- disliking exercise,

- finding it boring,

- being too tired, or

- overweight, or

- anxious/embarrassed, or

- busy, or...

- too old!

WHY MOVE?

If exercise could be packaged in a pill, it would be the single most widely prescribed and beneficial medicine in the nation.

Dr Robert H. Butler (Professor of Geriatrics, founder/CEO of the International Longevity Centre and author of *The Longevity Prescription*)

THE BAD NEWS IS...

... physical inactivity can, at worst, kill you. According to the World Health Organization, it is the fourth leading risk factor for global mortality, causing an estimated 3.2 million deaths each year.

THE GOOD NEWS IS...

... if you exercise regularly, you will feel and see positive benefits, both mental and physical. On a day-to-day basis you will feel better, have more energy, have fewer aches and pains, and be able to pick up something from the floor or get up from an armchair without grunting!

According to experts, regular physical activity:

1. reduces the risk of many major illnesses, including heart disease, stroke, Type 2 diabetes and many cancers, by up to 50 per cent,
2. lowers the risk of early death by up to 30 per cent,
3. keeps bodies stronger and more flexible,
4. increases stamina,
5. improves balance and helps prevent falls (a 36 per cent–68 per cent reduction in hip fractures),
6. increases well-being, self-esteem and energy,
7. improves cognitive function (including thinking, learning and memory),
8. reduces the risk of dementia/Alzheimer's or delays its onset,
9. prevents weight gain,
10. reduces stress, anxiety and depression,
11. improves sleep, which is also crucial for good health.

AND THE BEST NEWS IS...

... it's easy for most of us to become more active – and you can start immediately.

For example, a 12-year study found that people over 60 who walked for just 15 minutes a day reduced their risk of dying early by 22 per cent. Physical activity has been called *"the miracle cure"* by the UK National Health Service.

WHAT ARE WE ALL WAITING FOR?

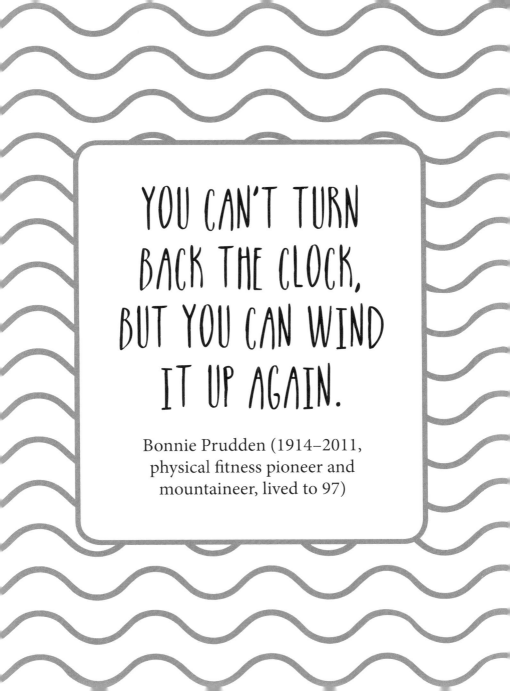

YOU CAN'T TURN BACK THE CLOCK, BUT YOU CAN WIND IT UP AGAIN.

Bonnie Prudden (1914–2011,
physical fitness pioneer and
mountaineer, lived to 97)

HOW MUCH IS ENOUGH?

There are global recommendations on physical activity for health (*including* for those who are over 65) that you should follow, unless you've had medical advice to the contrary:

- Every week do at least 150 minutes (for example 30 minutes, five times a week) of *moderate-intensity physical activity*. This will increase your stamina and cardiovascular (heart) health. *Moderate-intensity physical activity* is activity that makes you breathe faster (raising your heart rate) and feel warmer. You should be able to talk but not sing the words in a song. Even bouts of 10 minutes of moderate-intensity activity count towards the 150 minutes total.

- Alternatively, do at least 75 minutes of *vigorous-intensity activity* a week. *Vigorous-intensity activity* makes your heart beat rapidly, you breathe much harder, and you will be unable to carry on a conversation.

- You can do some *moderate-* and some *vigorous-intensity activity*.

- Twice weekly do exercise that increases the *muscle strength* of the legs, hips, chest, abdomen, shoulders and arms. We lose muscle mass and function as we age so maintaining strength is key.

- Exercise that improves *flexibility*, *suppleness* and *balance* is also recommended.

Stretching joints and strengthening muscles are extremely important as you age, enabling you to continue everyday activities (such as getting up from the toilet, getting dressed, climbing stairs) and so remain independent in later life. Retaining good balance is also vital, helping to prevent falls, which can have serious consequences for health and confidence.

But you'll no doubt be pleased to hear that *extreme* or *excessive* exercise provides no added benefits and may cause injuries.

Fitness can make the difference between dependence and independence.

Professor Sir Muir Gray (born 1944, physician, public health consultant, and author of several books, including *Sod 70!*)

Find an activity you enjoy, or it will be almost impossible to make it an integral part of your future life once the initial enthusiasm and motivation has worn off. Fortunately, there are so many options to try (as you'll see in the tips that follow) that there's bound to be at least one that suits you.

The more we do, the more we can do.

William Hazlitt (1778–1830, writer, and drama and literary critic)

TIPS

Ask not what your *body* can do for you, ask
what you can do for your *body*.
Slightly paraphrasing John F. Kennedy (1917–1963,
thirty-fifth US president), substituting "body" for "country"

TIP 1

Walking 10,000 steps a day, about 5 miles (8 km), is often recommended as a target. Although there is no scientific evidence for this suggested amount (and some recent research is now advocating 15,000 steps), it's still a good guideline to aim for. It's easy to measure your step count by wearing a pedometer (which can be bought fairly cheaply) or activity tracker, or by using a smartphone app. Ambling for 10,000 (or even 15,000) steps will not meet the moderate-intensity activity target referred to above, BUT it is much better to walk at any pace than not at all.

TIP 2

Brisk walking (3–5 mph/5–8 km/h) is an ideal aerobic, *moderate-intensity* exercise for increasing heart health and stamina. It's free, requires no specialist equipment or location, can be combined with other pleasurable activities (such as listening to music or chatting to friends), and has the advantage of getting you to where you need to go! Walking outdoors, especially in nature, also improves mood and decreases stress. You have the added bonus that being out in the sun is good for you – so long as you don't burn. It provides vitamin D that protects against many diseases, including osteoporosis/fragile bones. You will probably know how sensitive your skin is and, clearly, it depends on the strength of the sun, but it's recommended that after 10–20 minutes you apply sunscreen to avoid skin damage, wrinkles and, at worst, skin cancer.

So, get off the bus a stop or two earlier. If you have a car, try using it less and walk to public transport or park a little further away. Go for a walk in your lunch hour rather than sitting at your desk. Get a dog – great for regular exercise and good for meeting people and companionship. Make a start with a 10-minute brisk walk daily and build up from there.

> **Walking is the best possible exercise.**
> **Habituate yourself to walk very far.**
> Thomas Jefferson (1743–1826, third US president)

TIP 3

Household chores, such as vacuuming, scrubbing the floor or bath, or washing a car, can be *moderate-intensity* activities if they raise the heart rate, making you breathe faster. Vacuuming is also good for strengthening arms, legs and core muscles – put on some upbeat music and you'll increase the pace. Housework is not everyone's favourite occupation so it may be motivating to know it is benefitting you as well as your home.

TIP 4

Gardening can be a *moderate-intensity* activity if you are mowing, weeding, raking and planting (and not just watering the flowers!). Digging counts as *vigorous* activity. And vigorous gardening is also *muscle-strengthening*. Although pottering around the garden may only be light activity, it's better than nothing and will still improve your health.

TIP 5

Other day-to-day activities, such as climbing stairs and moving heavy loads are, unsurprisingly, *vigorous* activities. And if you also walk up escalators you can feel rather smug overtaking those – many younger than you – who let the escalator do all the work! Carrying heavy bags of shopping is also *muscle strengthening*.

TIP 6

Swimming is good *moderate-* or *vigorous-intensity* aerobic exercise, depending on the stroke and speed. It's a great choice for all-round exercise as it provides a full body workout, while *building muscle strength* and improving *balance* and *flexibility*. And it's low impact, avoiding stress on the joints. If you can't swim, try some lessons or water aerobics where you can stay within your depth.

The water does not know your age.
Dara Torres (born 1967, 12 times Olympic medalist and, at 41, oldest swimmer in the US Olympic team)

TIP 7

Exercise classes (many specifically for older people), run by community centres, gyms, studios, charities and others, can be very helpful for safe instruction, supervision, sustaining motivation, social connection and fun! There is also an increasing variety of dance-based fitness classes (such as Zumba), if you are reasonably active, which some people find more enjoyable. Or, even better, become a fitness instructor or sports volunteer and inspire others.

TIP 8

Weight training and using resistance bands count as *muscle-strengthening* exercises.

TIP 9

Pilates, yoga, T'ai Chi and Qigong (or Chi Kung) are *muscle-strengthening* exercises that also improve *flexibility, suppleness and balance*, reducing the risk of falls. Yoga, T'ai Chi and Qigong have multiple benefits for both body and mind (including heart health and improved mood) and are a great choice for those unable to do more vigorous exercise. They come in many forms but all focus on breathing and physical movement. Some forms of yoga are more vigorous; others have a greater emphasis on meditation. A newcomer might wish to start with a beginner's general "hatha yoga" class rather than, say, Bikram ("hot") yoga where the room temperature is around 35–42 °C (95–107 °F).

TIP 10

Dancing is highly recommended and many people's exercise of choice (mine included). Doctors can already prescribe dancing in some enlightened areas in the UK and it's likely to become more widely available with the growth of social prescribing. Dance classes for those with Parkinson's disease, disabilities and dementia are increasing. Dancing ticks all the boxes, most styles improving *heart health, stamina, muscle and bone strength, flexibility, balance* and *co-ordination*, as well as improving well-being. Even better, studies show that regular dancing reduces the risk of dementia more than any other exercise. There are many different styles, from ballet to breakdancing, with classes available for older people – including total beginners. As a rough guide, ballroom and line dancing count as *moderate-intensity* exercise and dances such as jive, swing and the Charleston constitute *vigorous-intensity* exercise. (See **Step 4: Connect** and **Step 5: Grow.**)

> **You live as long as you dance.**
> Rudolf Nureyev (1938–1993, ballet and contemporary dancer)

TIP 11

Aerobic exercise classes (such as step classes), running, cycling fast/uphill, singles tennis and football are all *vigorous* activities. Some *vigorous* activities, for example, **circuit training or volleyball**, also provide *muscle-strengthening* requirements – two for the price of one.

TIP 12

Go to a local gym and/or, if the budget can stretch to it (good ones do not come cheap), try a few sessions with a **personal trainer**. There are also some single-sex gyms, so look to see if there's one near you if that appeals to you more.

TIP 13

Join activity groups for older people. They can be found online, through social media, or perhaps advertized at your local library (if you still have one). Some health charities, or those involved with older people, offer activities such as rambling, community gardening or walking football. Or try "parkrun" – a worldwide organization providing free weekly 5-km timed runs. You can walk, jog, run or simply volunteer.

TIP 14

Exercise at home if you are self-motivated. It's free if you use chairs, walls and tin cans as weights. Or buy aids such as resistance/exercise bands, dumb-bells, or, if affordable, a Wii or an exercise machine. DVDs, YouTube videos, podcasts, social media, and a vast choice of books and articles can help to motivate you and teach you how to do different exercises both correctly and safely.

The secrets of success are to:

- **Build activity into your daily life**. *Any* activity is better than no activity. More is better still. Even short bursts of gentle activity add up and may increase your chances of living longer. Forget "putting your feet up" and keep moving.

- **Limit sedentary behaviour**. Excessive sitting or lying is bad for your health **even if you are being physically active to the recommended extent**. It causes negative biological changes in the body. Stand up and move every 30 minutes. Standing can lower your risk of serious health issues and burns more calories than sitting – using up about 50 calories an hour. So, when you don't get a seat on public transport, tell yourself it's doing you good!

- **Get enough (but not too much) sleep** – about 7 to 8 hours on average is best. Enough sleep is vital for good physical and mental health and well-being, reducing the risk of many serious, even fatal, diseases. (See more in **Step 5: Grow**.)

- **STOP smoking – if you are!** It's never too late. Stopping greatly improves your chances of a disease-free, mobile, happier old age. If you give up at 60, for example, it will add three years to your life.

> **Take care of your body. It's the only place you have to live.**
> Jim Rohn (1930–2009, entrepreneur, author and motivational speaker)

IN SUMMARY:

* Find physical activity that you enjoy (or you won't stick at it), and

* Just keep doing it (unless there are medical reasons not to).

STEP 2:
EAT RIGHT

> **Let food be thy medicine, and medicine be thy food.**
> Hippocrates (460–370 BCE, Greek physician
> and "father of modern medicine")

The world is getting fatter as well as older. In 2016, 1.9 billion adults worldwide (more than the population of China!) were *overweight* (for most adults, this is a Body Mass Index (BMI) of between 25 and 29) *or obese* (BMI of 30 or above).

With the growth of portion sizes, the constant temptations to eat and to eat more, and the prevalence of appealing, calorie-dense foods, all combined with increasingly sedentary lifestyles, demanding work patterns and high levels of stress, it is almost inevitable that many people will eat unhealthily and put on weight. Obesity-related diseases cost our society billions every year – and the costs will go on rising if no action is taken.

WHY EAT RIGHT?

Eating the right foods, in the right quantities, is crucial for good health. We need to maintain a healthy weight – neither over- nor underweight. Weighing too little (a BMI below 18.5) is also unhealthy.

Consuming more calories than you burn almost always results in weight gain. An average woman generally needs around 2,000 calories a day and an average man around 2,500 to maintain weight. Many consume more than that, and some a *lot* more.

Obesity reduces life expectancy by an average of three to ten years. Being obese increases the risk of serious diseases, including cardiovascular (heart) disease, stroke, musculoskeletal diseases and many cancers. Obese adults are five times more likely to develop Type 2 diabetes than those of a healthy weight. And obesity can also adversely affect well-being and mental health.

Japan currently has the highest life expectancy in the world and the Japanese province Okinawa exceeds Japan's national average for longevity. The traditional "Okinawa Diet" is based on fewer calories (under 2,000 a day) than the rest of Japan and includes a very wide variety of foods, at least five servings of fruit and vegetables daily and limited sugar and salt.

The World Health Organization tells us what constitutes a healthy diet – a variety of foods, including fruits and vegetables (five portions a day), nuts and whole grains, and only limited amounts of salt, sugars, and fats.

Many countries, including the USA, have produced their own, broadly similar, dietary guidelines. For example, in the UK, the National Health Service recommends:

- **Fruit and vegetables**: at least five servings a day, probably more, to provide vital vitamins, minerals and fibre. It should be over one-third of what we eat daily. (Potatoes don't count.)

- **Starchy carbohydrates**: bread, rice, cereals, oats, pasta and potatoes should be just over one third of our daily food. Wholegrain or wholemeal is best. They provide fibre, vitamins and minerals.

- **Protein**: is essential for the body to grow and repair itself, for example, tofu, beans, pulses, nuts, seeds, poultry, fish (at least one portion a week of oily fish such as salmon, sardines or mackerel), lean meat and eggs. These foods also contain vitamins, minerals and fibre.

- **Milk and dairy (or dairy alternatives)**: yoghurt, cheese or soya drinks (fortified with calcium) should be included as they are all good sources of protein and calcium.

- **Fluids**: drink six to eight 8-oz glasses (about 1.5 litres total) of non-alcoholic liquids a day – water, lower-fat milk, sugar-free drinks, tea and coffee all count.

> Life expectancy would grow by leaps and bounds if green vegetables smelled as good as bacon.
> Doug Larson (1926–2017, columnist)

Limit the amount of red **meat** (such as beef, lamb and even pork), and especially processed meats (such as ham, sausages, bacon and salami) to 70 g or less per day – this is equivalent to about three standard portions of meat a week. This will reduce the risk of bowel cancer and heart disease. Choose chicken, turkey or a plant-based alternative instead.

Restrict eating **sugar**, especially free sugars, which are those added to foods by the manufacturer, cook or yourself as well as the sugar in honey, syrups and fruit juices. And also cut down on foods containing **salt** and **fat** (especially saturated fat). Examples include pies, cakes, biscuits, sweets, chocolates, jam, crisps and most fizzy drinks. They are often "empty calories" with little or no nutritional value, and when they are consumed in excess, they can cause obesity and related diseases, including Type 2 diabetes. But many people find these foods addictive, especially when salt, sugar and fat are combined, as they are in many processed foods.

> It is easier to change a man's religion
> than to change his diet.
> Margaret Mead (1901–1978, cultural anthropologist and author)

There is evidence that about three to four cups of **coffee** per day (including decaffeinated coffee) are good for your health (reducing the risk of stroke, diabetes and more), and also that caffeinated coffee and **tea** can enhance memory. Green tea has been considered a health-giving drink for centuries and has been called the "anti-ageing beverage". Studies report multiple health benefits, although the amount you need to drink has not been settled yet (possibly two to five cups a day).

As for **alcohol** (which has a high calorie content and makes you eat more), too many people are drinking more than the published recommended guidelines of a maximum of 14 units per week (equivalent to, for example, less than seven small 175-ml glasses of wine spread over a week). Some research says there is no safe level of alcohol consumption for good health. Other studies say if you stick to the guidelines, and preferably choose red wine, you reduce the risk of heart disease and perhaps dementia as well. Having two to three alcohol-free days a week is recommended and easy to implement – or should be!

And it gets better. **Dark chocolate** (with at least 70 per cent cocoa, and less sugar) benefits your heart, mood and, possibly, your memory, if eaten in moderation – disappointingly, though, that's just a few squares a day.

If you suffer from a medical condition (such as diabetes or coeliac disease) or are allergic or intolerant to any food (for example, nuts or lactose), then these guidelines will need to be adapted appropriately, with professional help. Alternatively, you may be avoiding certain foods, for example, if you follow a vegetarian or vegan diet for personal or health reasons. Fortunately, shops and restaurants increasingly cater for specialist diets as awareness and diagnosis improves and demand grows. Health professionals, books (including recipe books), magazines and reputable websites (for example, those of the government, health services and charities) can provide useful advice and information for whatever diet you need to stick to.

ONE CANNOT THINK WELL, LOVE WELL, SLEEP WELL, IF ONE HAS NOT DINED WELL.

Virginia Woolf (1882–1941, writer)

TIPS

You do *not* need to do *all* of these 37 tips! Choose one or two that you feel
will do you the most good to start with – and then build up from there.

WHAT TO EAT

TIP 1

Stick to (mostly) healthy foods as a way of life, instead of dieting.
"Yo-yo dieting" – repeatedly losing and then regaining weight – is
bad for your health. Ignore any new diets that emerge (and they
will keep emerging, as the weight-loss industry is worth billions!)
and instead, as far as possible, try to eat the recommended foods,
in the recommended quantities, every day. You can then give up
saying "I am going on/I am on the so-and-so diet" – for good!

TIP 2

Banish fad diets. There have been countless crazy fad diets, including some restricted to one particular food or liquid, and some totally excluding particular nutrient groups, such as carbohydrates or fats. Such diets are almost always:

- unhealthy,
- unnatural,
- unsustainable,
- unsociable,
- unappealing, and usually
- unsuccessful in the longer term!

It is said that 95 per cent of those who lose weight by dieting regain it in one to five years. That is because diets are also:

- unfair!

They cause neurological and hormonal changes, including slowing down the metabolism (hence making it easier to gain weight) and decreasing willpower, thus sabotaging any real chance of long-lasting success.

Many people try the same diet on repeated occasions as well as any new ones that appeal and yet the number of people who are overweight or obese still continues to rise.

TIP 3

Avoid most processed foods as they can contain high levels of fat, salt, sugar and calories. These include "convenience foods" such as ready meals (which are often more expensive), savoury snacks (such as pies and sausage rolls) and processed meats (including ham, bacon and sausages).

TIP 4

Fill up with whole fruits (and vegetables). And only drink one glass (150 ml) per day of fruit juices or smoothies (fruit in liquid form only counts as one portion of your "five-a-day", however much you drink). Whole fruits are healthier as you will almost certainly eat fewer portions than are contained in a smoothie or fruit juice, and consume natural, rather than free, sugars as well as fewer calories. Whole fruits also contain more fibre (keeping you feeling fuller for longer) and are less damaging to your teeth. And, as eating takes more effort and time than drinking, you're more likely to feel you have eaten more and your stomach will have time to signal to your brain to let you know you've had enough. (See Tip 24.)

TIP 5

Choose grilled, baked or poached rather than fried food at home or when eating out, and try to **avoid butter- or cream-based sauces**. And **don't fill up on bread** before your food even arrives – so easy to do if you're hungry.

TIP 6

Eat nuts. There's evidence that eating 1 oz (28 g) of nuts daily (about the equivalent of nine Brazil nuts) can reduce your risk of serious disease and even help you to live longer. Nuts are filling and nutritious, and they make a great snack. But don't overdo it, as they are calorific. And take care to avoid salted nuts.

TIP 7

Keep healthy snacks (such as raw vegetables, fruit and those nuts) readily available at home and take them with you when you go out. They will help you to resist buying crisps or chocolate.

TIP 8

Allow yourself small treats – even daily, if you have the willpower to keep them small and a treat. Total denial is hard to maintain long term.

TIP 9

Don't keep unhealthy foods visible or in easy reach. Better still, don't keep them in the house at all. "Out of sight, out of mind," as the proverb goes.

TIP 10

Ask restaurants if they have information on the nutritional and/or calorie content. It can be illuminating and helpful in deciding what to eat.

TIP 11

Don't aim or expect to achieve perfection. We are human and many "bad" foods, savoury and sweet, taste delicious and are designed to be "moreish". Enjoy indulging occasionally and in moderation – and don't feel guilty! Tomorrow is another day.

> **All you need is love. But a little chocolate now and then doesn't hurt.**
> Charles M. Schulz
> (1922–2000, cartoonist and creator of *Peanuts*)

BUYING FOOD

TIP 12

Make a shopping list – and stick to it. Otherwise you'll probably come home with too much (possibly unhealthy) food.

TIP 13

Don't food shop on an empty stomach. The same applies. You will buy more, and unhealthier, foods.

TIP 14

Check food labels on packaged/processed foods for their calories, fat, sugar and salt content before buying. If the pack has colour-coded nutrition labels, follow the traffic lights and go green.

TIP 15

Ignore all unhealthy foods offered at the checkout tempting you to make impulse purchases. Your waistline, and wallet, will thank you.

> **I can resist everything except temptation.**
> Oscar Wilde (1854–1900, playwright and poet)

HOW TO EAT/ DRINK HEALTHILY

TIP 16

Eat a healthy breakfast. Research has shown that a well-balanced breakfast is good for health, weight maintenance, metabolism and mental performance. Many say it is the most important meal, as you've not eaten all night (assuming there have been no midnight feasts!). Eating protein keeps you feeling full for longer and you're less likely to reach for a mid-morning snack. Good choices include a poached or boiled egg with wholemeal toast. Porridge/oatmeal, wholegrain cereals, fruit, yoghurt, milk, coffee and green tea are all recommended and far preferable to a full English breakfast, waffles, pancakes or other high-fat, calorific foods.

TIP 17

Eat when you're hungry. Ignoring your hunger is likely to make you eat more, and more unhealthily, when you eventually succumb.

TIP 18

Drink regularly – what seems like hunger is often thirst. As mentioned, it is necessary to drink six to eight glasses every day (alcohol is not included!) to function, and even more in hot weather. Our bodies are about 50–60 per cent water. The elderly are especially susceptible to dehydration, which can become a serious problem. Feeling thirsty is a symptom. Keep some water with you when you go out and make sure you drink enough throughout the day.

TIP 19

Make meals attractive and colourful – "Eat the rainbow". You can mix and match vegetables or fruits and create highly colourful, nutritious salads. A healthy, multicoloured meal looks enticing, will be fresh and full of flavour, and is more likely to provide the varied vitamins and minerals you require.

TIP 20

Sit down to eat, if possible. We tend to eat more if standing and nibbling. A whole bowl of nuts or crisps can rapidly disappear, almost without us noticing. And we tend to forget, or discount, such eating.

TIP 21

Be mindful – notice and enjoy your food. If watching television, reading or using digital technology while eating, it's easy to be unaware of what, or how much, has been eaten. So, close the book or iPad and focus on what you're eating instead.

> One of the very nicest things about life is the way we must regularly stop whatever we are doing and devote our attention to eating.
>
> Luciano Pavarotti (1935–2007, operatic tenor)

TIP 22

Eat slowly, pause regularly and chew more. If you do, you'll realize how much you're consuming and how full you're becoming.

TIP 23

Visualize a stomach. It is pear-shaped and small, only about 12 inches (30.5 cm) by 6 inches (15.2 cm) at its widest, so it does not need a huge quantity of food to fill it. But, as we know, a stomach can stretch hugely!

TIP 24

Stop eating when you are beginning to feel full, but could still eat more. It takes about 20 minutes for the brain to register you are full after eating. If you feel full at the end of a meal, you've probably overeaten.

TIP 25

"Don't treat your stomach as a dustbin" the saying goes. For example, if there are leftovers it's all too easy and tempting to eat them, perhaps telling yourself you're not "wasting" food. But it all mounts up. Save them for tomorrow or use them in some other dish.

HOW TO LOSE WEIGHT
IF YOU NEED TO

TIP 26

Aim big (if necessary) but have small, achievable, short-term weight-loss goals. Persevere and believe you can lose weight. A weight loss of a pound or two a week is realistic and more likely to succeed and stay off. Think of the joke: Q. "How do you eat an elephant?" A. "In bite-sized chunks." Apply that approach to your weight-loss plan. And **celebrate success** – but not with chocolates!

> **You can break that big plan into small steps and take the first step right away.**
> Indira Gandhi (1917–1984, politician and Indian prime minister)

TIP 27

Weigh yourself regularly, every few days. **Keep a record.** Gaining a pound or two doesn't matter, but if the weight is slowly and steadily creeping up (and all your clothes seem to have shrunk!), it's time to act.

TIP 28

Reduce portion sizes. Try having your main meal on a dessert-sized plate which makes it look more – but don't cut out the healthy foods to fit it all on. You can buy special diet plates that are divided into sections to show the right quantities for each of the food groups. This can help, for example, to reduce the meat portion and increase the vegetable portions. Some restaurants provide one portion that could very easily feed two people. Share, or don't be afraid to leave some food on your plate – and get the leftovers bagged up to take away with you for another day. Or, order two starters instead of a starter and main course.

We never repent of having eaten too little.
Thomas Jefferson (1743–1826, third US president
and primary author of the Declaration of Independence)

TIP 29

Keep a food diary. Be truthful and write down everything you eat – it's so easy to discount (or to forget) the odd bag of crisps. It can be an unpleasant surprise to see in writing how much food we can get through in a single day.

TIP 30

Use technology – if that appeals. Apps or wearable devices can keep a record of calories eaten and burned, weight loss and more.

TIP 31

Join a weight-loss club that promotes healthy eating – many people find this helps with motivation and support. There are some "virtual" clubs online if there aren't any within easy reach of where you live.

TIP 32

Get support from friends or family – or, even better, get them to join you in eating healthily. Tell them what you are doing and ask them to keep an eye on your progress – it's harder to let things slide if others are aware of how you're getting on and their encouragement will help you to persevere.

TIP 33

Get advice. Examples of where to look include: books and articles by qualified professionals and health organizations; television programmes on healthy eating; and online sites and forums run by the government, health services, health insurance companies and medical charities. Or ask others how they maintain a healthy weight, or managed to both lose weight sensibly and to keep it off. But don't be seduced by any fad diet hype.

TIP 34

Go on a sponsored healthy-eating diet and raise money for your favourite charity.

TIP 35

Put three 1 kg bags (total 6.6 lbs) of sugar in a big bag tied around your waist for a couple of hours and keep moving, including climbing stairs. When you discard it, you'll realize how much difference carrying just a few extra pounds or kilos makes. This should help improve or maintain motivation. Just make sure you don't use the sugar to bake a cake afterwards!

TIP 36

Discover any overeating triggers you might have. For example, you might know that you tend to eat unhealthily when you are tired, stressed, bored, have sat for too long at the computer or watching television, or are in a low mood. If you don't know what the triggers are, you could try keeping a note of the occasions when you eat despite not feeling hungry and see if a pattern emerges. Then try to address the causes of this unhealthy eating rather than reaching for food – for example, go to bed earlier, meditate, distract yourself with a magazine, contact a friend, take a walk, or put on some good music and get dancing around your kitchen, not eating in it.

And finally, follow the other tips in this step – and the other steps in this book. You may find that they will also help you to eat more healthily, as you will feel fitter, busier, less stressed and happier. For example, **keeping active** will help to maintain weight, but you do need to do a significant amount of exercise to actually lose weight. (See **Step 1: Move**.) **Getting enough sleep** is, surprisingly, important in regulating how much we eat and avoiding obesity. (See **Step 5: Grow**.) And visualising a slimmer you and thinking positively about eating well will help you to achieve a healthier self. (See **Step 8: Be Positive**.)

> **If hunger is not the problem, eating is not the solution.**
>
> Anonymous

IN SUMMARY:

- ✫ Eat healthy foods,
- ✫ In moderate-sized portions
- ✫ Stop before you feel full, and
- ✫ Don't give up!

ONE SHOULD EAT TO LIVE, NOT LIVE TO EAT.

Molière (1622–1673,
French playwright and actor)

STEP 3:
HAVE A PURPOSE

> The afternoon of life is just as full of
> meaning as the morning; only, its
> meaning and purpose are different.
>
> Carl Jung (1875–1961, psychiatrist who lived to 85)

We all need something to live for, something that gives meaning and purpose to our lives and makes us want to get out of bed every morning. The Japanese, who have the longest life expectancy in the world, call it *"ikigai"* or a "reason for being" and attribute their increased longevity to this concept.

As we age, our priorities change and we may seek a new purpose; perhaps one less focused on children, earning a living, or success (however we define that). It may be time to consider how we wish to spend our later life, possibly making a greater contribution to others or to society. (See **Step 7: Give**.) There should also be some *"me time"* – having fun and spending time on what you love doing, or have always wanted to do, but never had the chance.

LIFE'S MOST PERSISTENT AND URGENT QUESTION IS "WHAT ARE YOU DOING FOR OTHERS?"

Martin Luther King Jr (1929–1968, minister and civil rights activist)

WHY HAVE A PURPOSE?

> **He who has a why to live for can bear almost any how.**
> Friedrich Nietzsche (1844–1900, philosopher)

Purpose is linked to living longer, an improved self-image and long-lasting well-being (as opposed to the short-term happiness gained from activities such as a good party or a longed-for new purchase).

> **An inordinate passion for pleasure is**
> **the secret of remaining young.**
> Oscar Wilde (1854–1900, playwright and poet)

Many studies have shown that having a strong purpose and sense of direction improve physical and mental health, and provide your brain with greater resilience to diseases, such as Alzheimer's, and minor cognitive problems.

It can also promote better sleep, which is crucial for health – so long as you're not lying awake thinking about all the things you plan to do the next day. (If so, see tips on sleep in **Step 5: Grow**.)

> **A man will never grow old if he knows what**
> **he's doing tomorrow and enjoys it.**
> Charles Aznavour (1924–2018, singer and lyricist; his last concert was held two weeks before his death at the age of 94)

TIPS

TIP 1

Discover what you want, what your goals are, and how to achieve them. You might already know, but, if not, talk to others and find out what they want to achieve (or have achieved) in their lives. This may give you some ideas and motivation. Or try some inspirational reading, biographies for example.

First say to yourself what you would be;
and then do what you have to do.
Epictetus (55–135 CE, Greek Stoic philosopher)

TIP 2

Write down your goals. Make them SMART – a useful acronym first created by management guru George Doran. It stands for:

- **S**pecific
- **M**easurable
- **A**chievable
- **R**ealistic, and
- **T**ime-bound.

For example, "work towards ending world poverty" is admirable but too vague. "Become a volunteer, within six months, for a charity helping the homeless" would be SMART.

If you want to live a happy life, tie it to a goal.
Albert Einstein (1879–1955, theoretical physicist)

TIP 3

Take action to try to achieve your goals. From time to time revisit and review them, to remind yourself and check they're still relevant and SMART. If they're not, then update them.

TIP 4

Don't rush to fill your days with fresh responsibilities and commitments on retirement. You may benefit from slowing down, reflecting and just *being* rather than doing. Some mental space will help you to clarify what you want and what gives your life meaning. If you give yourself time, you may discover you want your life to go in a new direction. (I did!)

By slowing down at the right moments, people find that they do everything better: they eat better; they make love better; they exercise better; they work better; they live better.
Carl Honoré (born 1967, journalist and author)

TIP 5

Keep working, if you can and if you enjoy it. Many get their purpose in life from their work. Research shows fulfilling work increases the chances of a good later life. Work can keep us physically and mentally active and also provide social connections, identity, status, achievement, independence, a sense of community, and a structure to our life. Hopefully, it will also provide financial security, although you can always offer your skills and experience without pay. (See **Step 4: Connect**.)

> **Never give up work. Work gives you meaning and purpose and life is empty without it.**
>
> Stephen Hawking (1942–2018, theoretical physicist, cosmologist and author still working at the time of his death, aged 76)

TIP 6

Seek flexible or part-time work, or consider a job-share, if you want or need to. It's a great way to keep working for longer, or as a way of transitioning into a delayed retirement. You will have more time and energy for the other steps in this book, such as keeping active and being sociable. Ask your employer or colleagues, neighbours or friends. Seek out local opportunities or try one of the growing number of online recruitment agencies that specialize in flexible working. The range and level of such jobs are steadily increasing. Driving, retail, hospitality and teaching are all well suited to part-time hours, if those jobs fit your skills and goals.

TIP 7

Start a new career or start your own business and be an entrepreneur. As well as finding a new purpose, you may reap financial rewards or gain new skills, interests, colleagues and friends. You could retrain by looking at an **apprenticeship** – some exist specifically for older people. Statistics show the fastest-growing group of entrepreneurs is aged 55–64 – and they tend to be successful. The wisdom and expertise accumulated over the decades can reap benefits in later life. Think about any business or other skills you've acquired, and your unique selling point (USP). What do friends ask you to help them with? What do they find difficult which you do not? Perhaps you could turn a hobby into a business. Then learn all you can, get advice and support from friends, family or a mentor, embrace technology, and be prepared for a lot of hard work! (See **Step 5: Grow.**)

TIP 8

Make it your purpose to help others. Volunteer. Everyone can help someone, for example, by offering their time, company, skills or care. Your experience could also benefit your local community, young people, or those less fortunate or less successful than you have been. It may even lead to paid work. (For examples of what you can do and how you can help, see **Step 7: Give**.)

> The purpose of human life is to serve, and to show compassion and the will to help others.
> Albert Schweitzer (1875–1965, theologian, philosopher and physician)

TIP 9

Join with others to help older people age better, whatever their income, gender or race. With populations ageing, we all need a world that values older people, "reframes" ageing and eliminates negative stereotypes. Decide to raise awareness of ageism in our society, change our culture or encourage social change in some way. Work, volunteer or campaign for good health and social care, financial security, suitable working practices, housing or products, or age-friendly communities. There are organizations, charities, focus groups, social media and more with which you can get involved and add your voice and lived experience.

> Never doubt that a small group of thoughtful, committed citizens can change the world; indeed it's the only thing that ever does.
> Margaret Mead (1901–1978, cultural anthropologist and author)

TIP 10

Find your passion(s):

- Think about what you enjoy doing now, and/or enjoyed when you were a child, or
- Think about what you've always wanted to try or dreamed about, but never had the chance, time, or courage
- Research your choice – the costs and available opportunities, and
- *Go for it!*
- Try lots of new things, if necessary – in time, you will find your passion, and you will have grown as a person and had fun in the process.

TIP 11

Develop your passion(s). When you have found something that calls to you, for example art, history, sport or activism, see how you can develop it. Look up local classes or online courses, or groups you can join in real life or on social media for advice, support and encouragement. Following your passion can significantly enhance your life, and maybe others' lives too. (See **My Story**, page 13 and **Step 5: Grow**.)

> Write, paint, sculpt, learn the piano, take up dancing, whether it's the tango or line dancing, start a college course, fall in love all over again – the possibilities are limitless for you to achieve your private ambitions.
>
> Joan Collins (born 1933, actress and author)

TIP 12

If you have a faith, take part in your religious community. Actively practising your religion gives life deeper meaning as well as offering many opportunities to help others in need. If you are non-religious, there are many humanist groups that can give your life purpose and inspiration, and the chance to help at a local or national level. (See **Step 4: Connect.**)

TIP 13

Don't let lack of money, or other obstacles, deter you from taking the first steps towards your goals. There may be ways of achieving your purpose with minimal resources or by seeking advice from others on how they got started. Start small if necessary, be ambitious and confident, but have realistic expectations. Believe in yourself and don't underestimate what you can achieve. Many highly successful ventures began on a kitchen table with little more than determination and passion.

> **If you truly pour your heart into what you believe in, amazing things can and will happen.**
>
> Emma Watson (born 1990, actress and activist)

TIP 14

Don't give up. Use failure to improve. Finding, working towards and hopefully achieving your goals may be quick and joyful, or may involve patience, failure, taking a risk or two, and being out of your comfort zone. Be prepared and positive, but content to fail. And, if necessary, seek inspiration. For example, Agatha Christie, one of the best-selling novelists of all time, had four years of rejections before getting her first novel published. Persevere.

> Let me tell you the secret that has led me to my goal. My strength lies solely in my tenacity.
>
> Louis Pasteur (1822–1895, biologist and chemist)

TIP 15

And finally, think about what you would like said about you at your funeral, or in your obituary, and if you haven't yet achieved it – **get started!**

> Think of yourself as dead. You have lived your life. Now take what's left and live it properly.
>
> Marcus Aurelius (121–180 CE, Roman emperor, Stoic philosopher)

IN SUMMARY:

For health, well-being and longevity:

✵ Make your life worth living - for you, and hopefully

✵ Worth your having lived - for others.

THE PURPOSE OF LIFE
IS NOT TO BE HAPPY.
THE PURPOSE OF LIFE
IS TO MATTER, TO BE
PRODUCTIVE, TO HAVE IT
MAKE SOME DIFFERENCE
THAT YOU LIVED AT ALL.

Leo Rosten
(1908–1997, humourist and political scientist)

STEP 4: CONNECT

The best thing to hold on to in life is each other.
Audrey Hepburn (1929–1993, actress, model and humanitarian)

Human connection lies at the heart of human well-being. At the end of our lives, we usually realize (if we hadn't before) that it is the people we care about that matter most, not our career or possessions.

But as we age, many transitions and changes, often outside our control, can leave us isolated or lonely. For example, the loss of friends or family, giving up work and colleagues, caring responsibilities, disability, physical or mental health conditions (which can reduce mobility, independence and motivation), financial hardship, transport difficulties, community facilities closing, living alone, moving away from those we know, our children having grown up and leading busy lives (or being out of reach), and digital exclusion. Such events can make it difficult to stay socially active and to make new friends.

WHY CONNECT?

Man is by nature a social animal.
Aristotle (384–322 BCE, Greek philosopher)

According to many experts, all ages are now suffering from a "loneliness epidemic" in the UK and US. Loneliness has been defined in many different ways but often as feeling sad because you are alone or having social contacts but not of the quality you'd like. What *is* agreed is being lonely is dangerous. The evidence is clear – it increases the risk of many diseases, affecting physical and mental health. Research has shown that lacking social connections is as damaging to our health as smoking 15 cigarettes a day. It is as big a killer as obesity, increasing the risk of premature death by about a third.

Being sociable and having good friends and family who we can count on not only improves our health and well-being but protects our brains, keeping our memory and cognitive function sharper for longer. Quality, not quantity, is what matters.

A 75-year-long study that followed over 700 men discovered that it was good relationships that keep us happier, healthier and living longer. Friends and family are also an important source of support, especially in tough times, helping to increase our resilience.

Connecting with others may therefore be the most important thing you do in life. And everyone can do it with knowledge, a little courage – and some help, if required.

TIPS

TIP 1

Develop and maintain strong family relationships. Cherish your parents, siblings, partner and children, if you have them. Grandchildren can also be a huge source of company, joy and self-worth; occasional (not full-time) care has been found to add years to your life. If your relationships are not what you would like them to be, can you make a move to improve them? Is it possible to build bridges, forgiving and forgetting any past hurts? (See **Step 7: Give**.)

There is only one happiness in life; to love and be loved.
George Sand (1804–1876, novelist and memoirist)

Friendship improves happiness and abates misery, by
the doubling of our joy and the dividing of our grief.
Marcus Tullius Cicero (106–43 BCE, Roman
philosopher, politician and lawyer)

Be a good friend. Do your best to be loyal, trustworthy, dependable, sociable, understanding, supportive and appreciative. Listen. Care. Spread joy, not negativity – monologues of complaint wear very thin after a time.

If friends are having a tough time, keep in regular contact through visits, telephone calls, text or email. Give practical help such as cooking a meal, offering to accompany them to medical appointments, or taking them to a funny film. You will benefit too. (See **Step 7: Give.**)

> A gentle word, a kind look, a good-natured smile
> can work wonders and accomplish miracles.
> William Hazlitt (1778–1830, writer and drama
> and literary critic)

Reconnect with "old" friends and former work colleagues you liked. You share history, ease and good memories. Write a letter or email if you're too shy to ring them up. See if they are on social media. Chances are they'll be delighted to hear from you. What have you got to lose?

> It is one of the blessings of old friends that
> you can afford to be stupid with them.
> Ralph Waldo Emerson (1803–1882, essayist,
> lecturer, philosopher and poet)

Have fun and laugh with others. This has a positive effect on building trust and developing communication. It is also a great way to connect and build relationships. (See **Step 8: Be Positive.**)

> **Laughter is the shortest distance between two people.**
> Victor Borge (1909–2000, comedian, conductor and pianist)

Make new contacts and develop new friendships. Be open, approachable and friendly (but sensible too, as scams aimed at older people do exist).

Incidental connections generate a sense of belonging. So be bold. Start conversations with people you come across (for example, in the bus or supermarket queue, sitting next to you in a class, or waiting for the doctor). You may need to make the first move and test the waters with a smile and light-hearted comment or question. You'll be surprised how just exchanging a few words with a stranger can improve your mood.

> **A friend may be waiting behind a stranger's face.**
> Maya Angelou (1928–2014, poet, author and civil rights activist)

Find opportunities to mix with other generations, for example, through local community and charity events, work or classes. Intergenerational contact has been shown to bring physical and mental benefits. (See **5. Grow**.)

> **Intergenerational solidarity is not optional, but rather a basic question of justice, since the world we have received also belongs to those who will follow us.**
>
> Pope Francis (born 1936, the 266th pope)

Keep working if you can, and if you want to. Apart from providing a purpose in life (as already mentioned), research shows that it is the social connections that people miss most when they stop working. (See **Step 3: Have a Purpose**.)

Volunteer – it is a great way to meet others with similar interests, make new friends and feel good. (See **Step 7: Give**.)

Engage in social, creative, cultural and physical activities. Start, or revive, a hobby. Join a community group, a choir, a book or arts club, or attend classes. Many activities are free or very low cost. You'll have an instant connection and topic of conversation with those who share your interests. Try a group for walking, foreign language conversation or games, where you can interact naturally, rather than following more individual pursuits. Or just make your hobby getting together regularly with friends, family or neighbours.

Your local council, doctors' surgery or library may have useful information, or you can look online. If you lack confidence, ask someone to go with you initially. Some organizations may provide a "buddy" to accompany you. Perhaps your doctor has taken up social prescribing (linking patients with community services and support). Research has shown that creative, cultural and social participation, and physical activity are all key contributors to well-being. (See **Step 3: Have a Purpose** and **Step 5: Grow**.)

> **Joy's soul lies in the doing.**
> William Shakespeare (1564 baptized–1616,
> playwright, poet and actor)

Join a gym with group classes and go to those you enjoy. It is more sociable than exercising alone on gym equipment. You'll get to know the regular attendees and improve your physical and mental health through getting fitter – two for the "price" of one. (See **Step 1: Move.**)

Dance. It is thought that dance originated as a form of "social glue" and it has been practised by every culture throughout human history. It is a great way to connect with others (often literally!) and make friends. Touch is the ultimate connection between two people, and partner dancing, or any dance that involves some physical connection, is beneficial to physical and mental health. People normally swap partners during classes or social dances, so you can go alone, although dancing with total strangers does take a little getting used to. There are classes for total beginners of all ages, and even some dance companies that give older people the opportunity to perform. Find details online by style of dance or location. You will feel more joyful after dancing in a group and that in itself will make it easier to connect with others. (See **My Story,** page 13 and **Step 1: Move.**)

> We should consider every day lost on which
> we have not danced at least once.
> Friedrich Nietzsche (1844–1900, philosopher)

TIP 12

Use the internet and social media to connect with friends, family and the rest of the world. If you are not already online (or you think a tablet is what you take every morning with food), learn to use digital technology. There are many books aimed at "seniors" that teach in "easy steps", or ask a friend to teach you. The basics are easy to master with help. Low-cost or free IT classes for older people are steadily increasing and can be found at libraries as well as local community centres and charities. (See **Step 5: Grow**.)

You will then be able to use email, Facebook, Skype or FaceTime (free video telephone calls), WhatsApp, texts and Twitter, to keep in touch with family, friends and others with similar interests, all over the world. There are online forums and social networking sites dedicated to all kinds of interests, topics and age groups, including ones for grandparents and older people. Your neighbourhood may have its own Facebook page, and there are likely to be Twitter accounts publicising what's going on locally and providing opportunities to get out, meet people and have fun. Research shows this sort of use of digital technology increases both physical and mental well-being in those over 80. It can make a huge positive difference, reducing isolation and enhancing quality of life. Technology is a very valuable addition for connecting with others, but it is not a complete substitute for actual face-to-face social interaction.

> **We are all now connected by the internet,**
> **like neurons in a giant brain.**
> Stephen Hawking (1942–2018, theoretical physicist,
> cosmologist and author)

Try dating or matchmaking agencies, if you're looking for a new relationship. There are some for the over-fifties, or for those with specific interests, backgrounds or faiths. Many are online. It is now one of the most common ways to meet a partner and is usually very safe. Another source is a newspaper's dating website, and local newspapers often have personal ads too. Take sensible precautions (such as meeting first in a public place and being alert to scams). There is advice online if you are interested. You are never too old for a new relationship.

Look – if he dies, he dies.

Joan Collins (born 1933, actress and author), said at age 69, on being asked about the age difference on marrying a man in his thirties

Choose holidays that cater for single travellers if you want to, or have to, go alone. (Some companies specialize in an older clientele if you would prefer that.) Group coach tours can be sociable. Walking, dancing, spa or "healthy living" breaks often welcome solo guests. If resources stretch to it, try cruising. It's easy to meet people at meals, activities and on excursions. Search for "solo" or "single holidays" online – another reason to develop IT skills. (See **Step 5: Grow**.)

To travel is to live.

Hans Christian Andersen (1805–1875, author)

Use charities that can help. They may have:

- Social groups and activities.
- Written material or online information and ideas, for example, for social activities or learning opportunities elsewhere.
- Befriending services (usually ongoing one-to-one companionship) if you are reluctant or unable to join a group.
- Regular telephone contact. Or free confidential helplines, which are usually open 24 hours a day, every day of the year.
- A local support group. If you have a medical condition, the charity relating to that condition (there's almost always at least one) may have local meetings. These can provide social connections as well as support and information on how to manage and live as well as you can.

Get out of your home if you think you're spending too much time there. Visit shared public spaces such as a museum or gallery (many are free), cinema (some have discounted showings for seniors), a concert, street market, library or park. Go with a friend or acquaintance, or alone if need be. Accept invitations even if you don't much feel like it. You never know who you might meet and, even if you don't, you will probably benefit from a new experience, improve your mood and get some exercise.

Access free or subsidized community transport services, if available and getting out and about is a problem. Senior travel discounts help reduce costs, or you could look into reputable car-/lift-sharing networks. Cycling Without Age enables older people to go out in "trishaws" (tricycle rickshaws) pedalled by volunteers (including older people). It now exists in 40 countries; if there aren't any near you, but it appeals, details are online of how to get a group started.

Attend religious services if you have a faith. It is a social community with opportunities to meet fellow congregants. Volunteer at your place of worship. Research has shown that those who have a faith live longer. (See **Step 3: Have a Purpose**.)

And finally, think about retaining and making new social connections into old age and whether that affects where you live in later life (assuming you have a choice and resources allow). Plan ahead. Do you want, or need, to downsize? Would "home-sharing" appeal — it could make use of available space, provide companionship and perhaps bring in extra income? A cottage deep in the countryside may sound ideal upon retiring, but will it provide those all-important social connections? Are you dependent on having a car and will you continue to be fit to drive? Alternatively, a retirement village or community may be highly attractive, where you can live alongside like-minded people, ready-made social opportunities and possibly health care – but, then again, it might be the last place where you would want to live, preferring an intergenerational or more urban environment. If you are living in a city, do your home and local area enable you to live healthily, safely and get out to meet others? A relatively recent, growing, trend is "co-housing", where people own their homes but share and manage communal spaces, organize activities and provide mutual support. Some exist solely for older people. Although not everyone will want, need, or be able to move, it's something to consider when thinking about how to make the most of your later years and maintain your well-being.

> **The ornament of a house is the friends who frequent it.**
> Ralph Waldo Emerson (1803–1882, essayist, lecturer,
> philosopher and poet)

IN SUMMARY:

Connecting with others and developing good relationships are key to health and well-being.

To connect:

- ✸ Begin!
- ✸ Be brave
- ✸ Befriend and
- ✸ Belong.

ALONE, WE CAN DO SO LITTLE; TOGETHER WE CAN DO SO MUCH.

Helen Keller (1880–1968, deaf-blind author, political activist and lecturer)

STEP 5:
GROW

Live as if you were to die tomorrow, learn as if you were to live forever.

Mahatma Gandhi (1869–1948, the leader of the Indian independence movement)

This step does not refer to growing vegetables or your bank balance, but to growing, enriching and exercising your mind through **lifelong learning**. You are never too old, and it is never too late, to learn new things, whether through formal education (a certificate, qualification or degree), or "DIY".

There are enormous numbers of people well past pension age acquiring knowledge, skills, businesses and interests. For some famous achievements, see **It's Never Too Late**, page 148.

WHY GROW?

> **Anyone who stops learning is old, whether at 20
> or 80. Anyone who keeps learning stays young.**
> Henry Ford (1863–1947, industrialist and founder
> of the Ford Motor Company, he lived to 83)

As we age, we may believe we have seen it all, or at least enough to know what we like and want to do now. This brings the risk that our behaviour and thinking may become narrow and inflexible.

Knowing and being comfortable with yourself, and what you want, are advantages of ageing. But being flexible and open to trying something new broadens knowledge and keeps us young.

> **It is not death that a man should fear, but he
> should fear never beginning to live.**
> Marcus Aurelius (121–180 CE, Roman emperor,
> Stoic philosopher)

Lifelong learning and new experiences also help us to have fun and stay involved in life. We can find a new purpose, skill, interest or perhaps a fresh career. It helps our confidence and creativity, makes us happier, and can even increase longevity.

> A person needs new experiences. They jar something deep
> inside, allowing you to grow. Without them it sleeps –
> seldom to awaken. The sleeper must awaken.
>
> Frank Herbert (1920–1986, science fiction writer,
> quote from *Dune*)

The expression **"use it or lose it"** applies to the mind as much as to the body. Exercising the brain by keeping your mind active, challenged and stimulated, especially by doing *new* things, helps prevent cognitive decline and reduces the risk of developing dementia. We need to make neural connections in our brains, as well as social connections in our community.

And learning will help provide those social connections too: for example, through courses, activities or sharing what we've learned. We meet people, make new friends and, as a result, reduce loneliness and isolation, which are so damaging to good health. (See **Step 4: Connect**.)

> A mind that is stretched by a new experience
> can never go back to its old dimensions.
>
> Oliver Wendell Holmes Jr (1841–1935, jurist and
> US Supreme Court judge until 90 years old)

TIPS

TIP 1

Try new things, and more creative activities, regularly. Research has shown there is a link between continued creativity and successful ageing, as it encourages motivation, develops problem-solving skills, and fosters a sense of competence, purpose and growth. So many options are available, from A(rt) to Z(umba). Write, paint, learn a musical instrument or digital photography, or even try creating a computer game or app. Regularly learning poems you like by heart has recently been found to benefit the brain. Do whatever you enjoy. Have a go at something you've never attempted before. For example, try **dancing**, where you can regularly learn new steps and also try dance styles that require quick decision-making. Now is the time to take up the wonderful Argentine tango! Dancing has been called a "cognitive wellness strategy", reducing dementia risk, keeping you physically and mentally well, making you happy and connecting you with others. (See **My Story**, page 13, **Step 1: Move**, **Step 3: Have a Purpose** and **Step 4: Connect**.)

I don't want to be told I'm too old to try something…
Let me have a go. Let us all have a go.
Dame Judi Dench (born 1934, actress)

TIP 2

Find your "flow". This concept, according to positive psychology founder Mihaly Csikszentmihalyi and others, is a key to happiness, creativity and productivity. It occurs when a person's body or mind is challenged (but not beyond their skill level), while they are doing something they enjoy. They become "in the zone", focusing totally in the moment, losing sense of self and time. It can happen, for example, when writing, playing sport, cooking, painting, dancing and working, but it takes practice. Try it for at least half an hour. "Flow" is the opposite of multitasking (doing more than one thing at a time or, more accurately, switching rapidly from one task to another). Multitasking is increasingly prevalent with the wide use of social media and digital technology, but it can negatively affect cognition and productivity. So, for "flow", all distractions need to be eliminated, including phones and emails.

> **True happiness comes from the joy of deeds well done, the zest of creating things new.**
> Antoine de Saint-Exupéry (1900–1944,
> writer, poet and pioneering aviator)

Learn another language if that interests you. This has been proved to be excellent for brain health, and for reducing the risk of dementia. It also broadens your understanding of other cultures, as well as providing practical benefits when on holiday abroad or if you retire to sunnier climes. For those at home it gives, for example, the satisfaction of being able to get to know a wider range of people, reading a book in its original language, or watching a foreign film without distracting subtitles. You will also meet new people if you join a group language class.

> **A different language is a different vision of life.**
> Federico Fellini (1920–1993, film director and screenwriter)

Take up a new career or job, set up a business, become a social entrepreneur, mentor or volunteer. Put your passion, skills and experience to good use. Books, courses, websites, forums, networks and friends can help. You may even make your fortune and/or make a positive difference to others. This tip will help you to grow as well as to have a purpose, so it is repeated here (see **Step 3: Have a Purpose**). It also contributes strongly to some of the other steps.

> **Start where you are. Use what you have. Do what you can.**
> Arthur Ashe (1943–1993, professional tennis player)

TIP 5

Believe that you can achieve new things, even late in life. We all can. Self-belief works. And you don't need perfection. Good is good enough. (See **Step 8: Be Positive** and **It's Never Too Late**, page 148.)

> *If you hear a voice within you that says "you cannot paint",*
> *then by all means paint, and that voice will be silenced.*
> Vincent van Gogh (1853–1890, Post-Impressionist painter)

TIP 6

Don't worry if you struggle. Persevere. Learn from failure. As we age, we may find it harder to pick things up – and not just literally! People who never fail or make mistakes are unlikely to have tried anything new. You learn from mistakes, improve and grow. (See **Step 3: Have a Purpose**.)

> **Ever tried. Ever failed. No matter.**
> **Try again. Fail again. Fail better.**
> Samuel Beckett (1906–1989, novelist and playwright)

TIP 7

Read much – and read widely. Try different types of books: for example, biographies, travel writing, science fiction or poetry. And perhaps consider joining, or starting, a book club. You can challenge your memory and brain in discussion and putting forward your views, while also making new connections and friends. (See **Step 4: Connect**.)

> **Reading is to the mind what exercise is to the body.**
> Joseph Addison (1672–1719, founder of *The Spectator* magazine and the *Guardian*)

TIP 8

Use the internet to learn. It is the quickest, most up-to-date source to use to discover almost anything, instantly – from "How do you unblock a toilet?" and "Where can I learn to cook?" to "What is a black hole?" and "Who is Madonna?". Ask online and you'll find plenty of answers, although they can vary in value and reliability, depending on the source. Often there are helpful YouTube videos and links to further resources too. Digital technology also provides information and help on every aspect of daily living (including health, finance, employment, travel, local events and money-saving offers), making our lives easier, cheaper and more fun.

If interested in more formal, in-depth learning, there are many apps and websites that can help you master skills, such as Bluprint for crafts education or LinkedIn Learning for software, business and creative skills.

This century has seen the growth of MOOC (massive open online course) providers, such as edX, and FutureLearn. They host a huge number and variety of courses from universities, cultural institutions or other organizations around the world, and most of them are free! (See **Step 4: Connect.**)

> **Computers themselves, and software yet to be developed, will revolutionize the way we learn.**
> Steve Jobs (1955–2011, businessman, investor and co-founder of Apple)

TIP 9

Keep up-to-date with what's going on in the world. You will learn much and keep in touch with our ever-changing, and admittedly sometimes depressing, world. It may well put personal difficulties in perspective and help you to feel grateful for your good fortune. You might find a cause to support (such as what can be done about climate change, alleviating the plight of refugees or protecting endangered wildlife) or a new purpose in life. At the very least, you'll have something to talk about when you meet new people and can learn from each other. (See **Step 3: Have a Purpose**, **Step 4: Connect** and **Step 6: Be Grateful**.)

> **Plunge boldly into the thick of life, and seize it where you will, it is always interesting.**
> Johann Wolfgang von Goethe (1749–1832, writer and statesman)

TIP 10

Learn from younger – and older – generations about literature, politics, history, business, art, fashion and more. Everyone can teach us something. Young people will keep you up to date and help you to grow. A love of new music trends, blogging or perhaps a new venture might emerge. Spend time with very young children – nurseries linked with care homes, for example, are on the increase, as they are proving physically and mentally beneficial to both young and old. (See **Step 4: Connect**.)

> Now that I'm 91, as opposed to 90, I'm much wiser.
> Betty White (born 1922, actress and comedian)

TIP 11

Embrace change and learn from it. Change is guaranteed throughout life, whether desired or dreaded. Having a flexible and open attitude enables us to cope better, learn and move forward – far preferable to the ostrich (head in the sand) approach or hostility.

> Progress is impossible without change and those who cannot change their minds cannot change anything.
> George Bernard Shaw (1856–1950, playwright and political activist)

Spend money on experiences rather than possessions. Research shows that *doing* things makes us happier than *having* things. Experiences provide the excitement of anticipation, the joy of the event, great memories – and far too many photos!

The soul's joy lies in doing.
Percy Bysshe Shelley (1792–1822, poet)

Travel. Or take a gap year (or months). Travel, at its best, is a shortcut to seeing life anew, expanding the mind, experiencing difference, increasing tolerance, and discovering our incredible world, its history and its cultures. Have an adventure off the beaten track, learn a language in its country of origin, or do voluntary work overseas. There are many companies (some catering especially for older people) that arrange such trips.

**Knowledge of the past and of the places of the Earth
is the ornament and food of the mind of man.**
Leonardo da Vinci (1452–1519, artist and
Renaissance polymath)

TIP 14

Do brain games, such as Sudoku, crosswords and other puzzles, if you enjoy them. You will learn and improve your performance in those activities, and many get huge satisfaction from completing them.

TIP 15

Do small things differently, to stop functioning on autopilot and help your brain health. Challenge yourself a little at fairly regular intervals. For example, try a new recipe, choose a different route to walk to work or to the shops, use a different hand to brush your teeth or eat with – you might find you eat less too!

TIP 16

Stay curious and keep learning how to live. Ask questions, listen to points of view you disagree with, challenge your beliefs and play devil's advocate. It will keep you feeling younger, more involved in life and stimulate your mind.

TIP 17

Avoid excessive television, time online and social media. Be active, not passive. Television (and digital technology) won't "rot your brain", as is often alleged, and they can be wonderful sources of connection and information when used purposefully. But it is worth remembering that these are sedentary and often solitary activities and that excessive or aimless time spent on a computer, tablet or phone is unlikely to benefit your health and mind. Experts have recommended a limit of one to two hours a day, and technology now exists to tell you how much time you have spent staring at a screen – from personal experience, the result can be both surprising and sobering! You could always watch television on a gym treadmill or while exercising at home instead. (See **Step 1: Move** and **Step 2: Eat Right**.)

> I find television very educational. The minute somebody turns it on, I go into the library and read a good book.
>
> Groucho Marx (1890–1977, writer, film star and comedian)

TIP 18

Have fun. Fun has been shown to improve our memory and concentration by reducing stress. Fun activities that introduce us to new ideas and concepts encourage learning and creativity. Play is good for healthy ageing. (See **Step 8: Be Positive**.)

> When you stop doing things for fun
> you might as well be dead.
>
> Ernest Hemingway (1899–1961, author and journalist)

And finally, get enough sleep (but not too much), and take naps. Sleep is vital for brain cells to work properly. Almost all adults should aim for at least seven hours' sleep every night. The recommendation is seven to nine hours. For most of us, too little (or poor quality) sleep increases the risk of a range of serious health problems (such as heart disease, diabetes and obesity), as well as memory problems and forgetfulness. Sleep deprivation also reduces how quickly we learn, solve problems, make decisions and process information, and our productivity can suffer. Feeling fresh and rested will make you more willing, ready and able to concentrate and learn. The cheering news is that evidence is mounting that naps of under 30 minutes (preferably in the early afternoon) can have important benefits for memory, learning, creativity, alertness and improving mood. *Viva la siesta!*

Unfortunately, many struggle with sleep in later life. If there is no medical cause for your insomnia (for example, medication or sleep apnea), there are things you can try to improve the quality and quantity of your sleep:

- Go to bed and get up at the same time every day to help your biological clock.
- Have a bedtime routine, for example, reading (though avoid thrillers), having a warm non-caffeinated drink or meditating.
- Stop looking at smartphones and laptops one or two hours before bed as the screen light can slow production of your sleep hormone (melatonin), and hinder relaxation.
- Avoid a large meal, caffeine or alcohol for several hours before bedtime. Any of these can stop you falling (or staying) asleep.
- Do not exercise during the two to three hours before your

bedtime as it may increase alertness – but exercising earlier in the day reduces stress, tires you out and promotes sleep.

- Avoid daytime naps of more than 30 minutes and avoid naps of any length from late afternoon onwards.
- Keep the room cool, dark and quiet (use eyeshades or earplugs if necessary). If your partner's snoring regularly keeps you awake, see if anything can be done, or consult your doctor. For example, sleeping position, alcohol consumption and being overweight can all cause (or increase) snoring. Many people resort to separate bedrooms to get the sleep they need.
- Listen to a progressive relaxation CD, app or download, or to music intentionally produced to aid relaxation. Try slow, deep breathing or tensing and relaxing each muscle group of the body from head to toe.
- Write down your next day's "to-do" list to help stop you from thinking about it in bed. Keep a pen and paper by the bed to note down anything important if you wake, so you can stop worrying whether you will have forgotten it by the morning.
- Do not check the time if you wake up as it can make it harder to get back to sleep.
- If you really cannot sleep, get up, walk around and do something boring (not checking your phone) for half an hour and then try to get (back) to sleep.
- Try keeping a gratitude journal (and see **Step 6: Be Grateful**).
- Laugh more – it relaxes muscle tension, reduces anxiety, helps to treat insomnia and improves sleep quality (see **Step 8: Be Positive**).

And, if you are lucky enough to have no such problems, don't sleep for too long – nine hours or more per night has also been found to be bad for health.

SLEEP THAT KNITS UP THE RAVELLED SLEEVE OF CARE... SORE LABOUR'S BATH, BALM OF HURT MINDS... CHIEF NOURISHER IN LIFE'S FEAST.

William Shakespeare (1564 baptized–1616, playwright, poet and actor)

IN SUMMARY:

✧ Be interested, informed, inspired and above all

✧ Be involved... in life and lifelong learning.

✧ You will stay sharper, happier and healthier, and

✧ Who knows what you might achieve!

THERE IS A FOUNTAIN OF YOUTH; IT IS YOUR MIND, YOUR TALENTS, THE CREATIVITY YOU BRING TO YOUR LIFE AND THE LIVES OF PEOPLE YOU LOVE. WHEN YOU LEARN TO TAP THIS SOURCE, YOU WILL HAVE TRULY DEFEATED AGE.

Sophia Loren (born 1934, film actress)

STEP 6:
BE GRATEFUL

Joy springs from a grateful heart.
Pope Francis (born 1936, the 266th pope)

Gratitude is defined as the appreciation of what is valuable and meaningful to oneself; it is a general state of thankfulness.

If we are lucky, we will live until we are old. We are privileged to have the gift of longer life and, perhaps, to have lived in better health than most who have gone before us. Older age can also bring time, freedom, wisdom, experience, perspective, fewer responsibilities, growth and confidence about who we are and what's important. For all this we can be grateful and happy – and we are, according to research.

Of course, getting older brings its own challenges, as does each stage of life. We, or those we love, may suffer ill health, we are likely to lose family and friends, and our financial security may be reduced. We also live in a culture that values youth and beauty and where ageism exists. Therefore, it may be hard to feel grateful at times. But it is good to remember that many who survive life-threatening events or illnesses report their appreciation of life is hugely enhanced. How much better it is to achieve this without suffering such trauma!

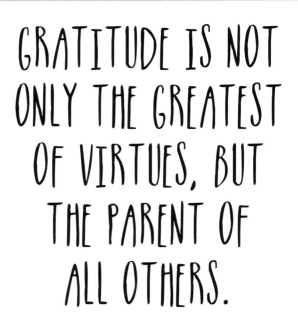

GRATITUDE IS NOT ONLY THE GREATEST OF VIRTUES, BUT THE PARENT OF ALL OTHERS.

Marcus Tullius Cicero (106–43 BCE, Roman philosopher, politician and lawyer)

WHY BE GRATEFUL?

Studies have shown that being grateful is extremely good for you, delivering benefits to your health, emotions, social life, personality and career. Gratitude can improve your:

- happiness and well-being – it's a "neural antidepressant", boosting the brain's endorphins or "happy chemicals";
- satisfaction with life (less envy of others and less materialism);
- physical health and immunity against disease;
- self-esteem and confidence;
- optimism;
- energy and willingness to exercise;
- mental strength and resilience;
- stress reduction;
- relaxation and sleep;
- sociability;
- relationships and friendships;
- empathy, kindness and helpfulness to others;
- attitude to work; and
- longevity.

That's more than most medicines – and there are no unwanted side effects.

TIPS

When you arise in the morning, think of what a precious
privilege it is to be alive – to breathe, to think, to enjoy, to love…
Marcus Aurelius (121–180 CE, Roman emperor, Stoic philosopher)

TIP 1

Learn and practise having an attitude of gratitude. Make it a
habit. It does not just happen, unless you're lucky. As with almost
everything, if you practise (for example, by following these tips),
you will improve.

Cultivate the habit of being grateful for every good thing
that comes to you, and to give thanks continuously.
Ralph Waldo Emerson (1803–1882, essayist, lecturer,
philosopher and poet)

TIP 2

**Count your blessings. Value what you have, rather than what
you lack. Take pleasure in what you can do, rather than what you
cannot.** There's always something to be thankful for. And however
bad things feel, they could almost always be worse.

He is a wise man who does not grieve for the things
which he has not, but rejoices for those he has.
Epictetus (55–135 CE, Greek Stoic philosopher)

TIP 3

Be grateful for your friends and family and tell them how much they mean to you. Write letters of thanks. Express your gratitude regularly. Giving thanks has a positive impact on both giver and receiver. (See **Step 7: Give**.)

> **We must find time to stop and thank the people who make a difference in our lives.**
> John F. Kennedy (1917–1963, thirty-fifth US president)

TIP 4

Be aware of, and take a moment to appreciate, simple pleasures and small things – a sunny day, a good song, someone's kind words or a meal with friends. Those reaching the end of their lives often say these are what really count.

> **To be content with what we possess is the greatest and most secure of riches.**
> Marcus Tullius Cicero (106–43 BCE, Roman philosopher, politician and lawyer)

TIP 5

Value each and every day you are alive, and make it count. Be grateful for another chance to enjoy life, do better, be different or start afresh. (See **Step 8: Be Positive.**)

> **Yesterday is history, tomorrow is a mystery. But today is a gift. That is why it is called the present.**
> Eleanor Roosevelt (1884–1962, political figure and activist)

TIP 6

Be grateful for who you are and proud of your achievements. List all your qualities and strengths. You will feel better, both mentally and physically.

> **To love oneself is the beginning of a lifelong romance.**
> Oscar Wilde (1854–1900, playwright and poet)

TIP 7

Remember and appreciate all the good things that have happened in your life. Write them down. Look at old photos. If we reflect on past, positive experiences, it has been found we are better able to enjoy life. You may be surprised at how much you have to be grateful for.

> **Let us remember the past with gratitude.**
> Pope John Paul II (1920–2005)

TIP 8

Be grateful to have reached the age you have. Many are not so fortunate. And value all the good things age has brought including (hopefully) more time, freedom and knowledge of what's truly important for a happy life.

> **No wise man ever wished to be younger.**
> Jonathan Swift (1667–1745, satirist, essayist and poet)

TIP 9

Keep a gratitude journal. Each night, write down three to five things that you are grateful happened during the day, whether large or small, such as starting a new book you've been waiting to read or even the bus arriving promptly. Studies have shown that noting and keeping such a record has many positive benefits.

TIP 10

Celebrate whenever there's a reason – however minor the reason. It's good for you. And, if there's nothing in particular, just celebrate being alive.

> **Stop worrying about the potholes in the road and celebrate the journey.**
> Fitzhugh Mullan (born 1942, professor)

TIP 11

Do more of what you love whenever you can – it will help you to appreciate your good fortune and bring joy. Be a little selfish and treat yourself on a daily basis. For example, meet friends, watch a film you love (maybe the 1946 classic *It's a Wonderful Life*), have a relaxing bath, listen to your favourite music, go for a walk in a park or the countryside, or spend time on your hobby or passion. And note them in your journal!

> **Too much of a good thing can be wonderful.**
> Mae West (1893–1980, actress, comedian, singer and playwright)

TIP 12

And finally, be grateful for living now, in the twenty-first century. Although it may not always feel like it, our modern lives are easier, healthier, more fulfilling, more peaceful and longer than those of any previous generation. Not only should we be grateful for that, but also to all those who helped to make it happen.

> **Keep smiling because life is a beautiful thing**
> **and there's so much to smile about.**
> Marilyn Monroe (1926–1962, actress, model and singer)

> **Being old isn't something to deny or hush up or apologize for. Far from it. It's something to celebrate.**
> Virginia Ironside (born 1945, author, journalist and agony aunt)

IN SUMMARY:

Gratitude brings joy, health and longevity.
And there is so much to be grateful for, including:

- ✧ Life
- ✧ Health
- ✧ Friends and family
- ✧ Yourself
- ✧ Yesterday, today, tomorrow and
- ✧ Our wonderful world.

THE ROOT OF JOY IS GRATEFULNESS... IT IS NOT JOY THAT MAKES US GRATEFUL; IT IS GRATITUDE THAT MAKES US JOYFUL.

Brother David Steindl-Rast
(born 1926, Benedictine monk and
writer on gratefulness)

STEP 7: GIVE

**The meaning of life is to find your gift. The
purpose of life is to give it away.**
Pablo Picasso (1881–1973, painter and sculptor)

By the time you reach later life, you will have accumulated
skills, talents and experience. You are also likely to have more
time and energy (especially if you are following the steps
in this book). And, according to research, you'll probably be
feeling happier and more satisfied with life too. If you haven't
already begun, can there be any better time to give to others,
to yourself and to our world?

**How wonderful it is that nobody need wait a single
moment before starting to improve the world.**
Anne Frank (1929–1945, diarist)

WHY GIVE?

If you want happiness for a year, inherit a fortune. If you want happiness for a lifetime, help somebody else.
Chinese proverb

Of course, if you give, those on the receiving end will benefit. But research has shown positive changes also happen to those who help others. Givers become happier, more fulfilled and thankful, and feel better about themselves and more connected to their community. There is reciprocity in giving.

For example, in 2014 an analysis of 73 studies, carried out over 45 years, showed that volunteering (for about 2 to 3 hours a week) by those aged 50 or older improved both physical and mental health and was associated with increased longevity. And recent research has shown that it also helps to keep the brain young.

"Generativity" (a term coined in the 1950s by psychoanalyst Erik Erikson) means making your life count, generating good things, and nurturing and guiding younger people, by contributing to society and contributing to the next generation. It is the opposite of stagnation and is important for happy, healthy ageing.

No one is useless in this world who lightens the burdens of it to anyone else.
Charles Dickens (1812–1870, novelist)

TIPS

Do what you can, with what you
have, where you are.
Theodore Roosevelt (1858–1919, twenty-sixth US president)

TIP 1

Give of yourself to those close to you. "Charity begins at home", as the proverb goes. If you have a partner, give love, kindness, time, respect, support and space. Cherish family and close friends. Tell them how much you care for them – many people regret not having done so before it was too late. Keep in touch and visit. Be there in times of need and celebration. Pass on your experience, wisdom and love to any grandchildren. Such small regular actions add up to a life well-lived and may extend it too.

I've learned that people will forget what you
said, people will forget what you did, but people
will never forget how you made them feel.
Maya Angelou (1928–2014, poet, author and civil rights activist)

TIP 2

Give joy, compliments, laughter – and lots of hugs. Try to make everyone feel better for having met you. You will feel uplifted too. People are attracted to, and like to be with, people who make them feel good. Think how much better you feel after hearing great comedy.

And give hugs regularly. Hugging releases the feel-good hormone oxytocin, reducing stress, blood pressure and more. (See **Step 4: Connect** and **Step 8: Be Positive**.)

> The happiness of life is made up of the little charities of a kiss, or a smile, a kind look, a heartfelt compliment.
> Samuel Taylor Coleridge (1772–1834, poet, literary critic, philosopher and theologian)

TIP 3

Rejoice in others' achievements and good luck. Give them your heartfelt congratulations and celebrate with them. Try not to feel you have missed out or be envious of their good fortune, but instead share in their joy. You will feel better and, when your time comes, you will enjoy others being happy for you, because (as the Bible says) what you sow you will reap.

> Whenever you hear that someone else has been successful, rejoice... If you cannot practise rejoicing, no matter how long you live, you will not be happy.
> Thubten Zopa Rinpoche (born 1946, Nepali Lama, Buddhist teacher)

TIP 4

Volunteer. There are countless charities. Most are small but still achieve enormous things. Volunteer, and put your skills to good use or develop new skills. There are so many ways you can contribute, including working in a charity shop, being a museum guide, answering calls on a helpline, administrative work, or becoming a trustee. Investigate websites that list local charities and vacancies or find one you feel a connection with. They will welcome and value your help. Volunteering may also help you to find your purpose, connect with others, grow and be (more) grateful for what you have. (See **Step 3: Have a Purpose** and **Step 4: Connect**.)

> **We can't help everyone, but everyone can help someone.**
> Ronald Reagan (1911–2004, actor and fortieth US president)

TIP 5

Help your local community, for example, by helping out in local activities, becoming a school governor or magistrate, or taking part in local government. Look for opportunities online or in public places such as the town hall, the library or doctors' surgeries.

> **Do your little bit of good where you are; it is those little bits of good put together that overwhelm the world.**
> Desmond Tutu (born 1931, Archbishop, theologian and human rights activist)

TIP 6

Donate money or fundraise. Give what you can afford (however small) to causes you support. Regular donations may also bring benefits – for example, if you can afford it, becoming a "friend" or supporter of a museum or arts company can provide free, or discounted, events. Get involved in a sponsored walk, run or climb; or fundraise through a book or cake sale, an auction, or quiz night. Apart from helping to raise money for worthy causes, you'll feel better yourself, have fun, and connect with others, and you may also get fitter or even develop new skills. And, if you can, leave a legacy in your will.

> **No one has ever become poor by giving.**
> Anne Frank (1929–1945, diarist)

TIP 7

Share your wisdom, expertise or passions, whether recently acquired or long-standing, with all generations. Offer to give talks or lectures, perhaps to community groups or a local school. Start a vlog (video blog) or Twitter account to share your knowledge on fashion, music, crafts, cooking, travel for seniors... whatever your interest may be. Investigate "time banking" – an exchange system where you "deposit" your skills and "withdraw" equivalent time and help on what you need. It exists in 40 countries and is a good way to build social networks too. You could give your views (through market research, charities or focus groups, for example) on what older people want and need from housing, communities, cities, health care, products, design, workplaces, technology and more. This will enable us all to age better in future. (See **Step 3: Have a Purpose.**)

> *The wisdom acquired with the passage of time is a useless gift unless you share it.*
> Esther Williams (1921–2013, **actress** and swimmer)

Become a coach or mentor, particularly to younger generations – they are the future. Pass on your experience, helping to guide and develop others so that they can achieve their goals. You will both benefit. There are various coaching training courses. You could coach or mentor friends and family informally or set up a business. (See **Step 4: Connect.**)

> *The greatest good you can do for another is not just to share your riches but to reveal to him his own.*
> Benjamin Disraeli (1804–1881, twice UK prime minister)

Declutter your home and donate items to charity shops. It will raise money for charity and help to make it possible for others to get something at an affordable price – and you will feel both liberated and more in control. However, for most of us, this is something that is very hard to do. This may explain the ever-growing number of books on how to declutter. Try not to end up like me, owning most of them, adding to your clutter and being no nearer to taking that first step! Read, learn, and then *act*.

Or get someone to help you, a friend or professional (they exist, if resources allow). Alternatively, sell unwanted items on eBay or at a car boot sale and give some, or all, of the proceeds to charity. Taking action now will save a lot of work later on for your offspring when you die (hopefully at a very advanced age). But in the interests of family harmony, it's probably wise to check before emptying your home – especially if you're disposing of family members' belongings, however old or supposedly unwanted.

> **Happiness is a place between too little and too much.**
> Finnish proverb

TIP 10

Give to yourself too – you also deserve time, space and fun, especially if you are caring for someone else. Try, every day if you can, to do something you want to do – or even just to do nothing. Never feel guilty – remember the analogy: when flying you put your oxygen mask on before putting one on your child. You'll be better able to help others if you look after yourself.

> **As you grow older, you will discover that you have two hands, one for helping yourself, the other for helping others.**
> Audrey Hepburn (1929–1993, actress, model and humanitarian)

TIP 11

Sell the results of your new-found creativity – your art or bestseller – and give some of the proceeds to charity. (See **Step 5: Grow.**)

TIP 12

And finally, consider organ and/or tissue donation on your death. Leave a legacy of life. There is no age limit – organs from donors in their seventies and eighties have been successfully transplanted. The organs from one donor may save up to 8 lives and help as many as 50 people – and there are *thousands* waiting for life-saving organ transplants. Studies show that not only does it make donors feel good to know they are, or will be, saving, prolonging or improving the lives of the recipients, but it also helps grieving families, perhaps giving some meaning to their loss.

> Whoever saves a single life is considered
> to have saved the whole world.
> *The Talmud*

IN SUMMARY:

✫ Give what you can, when you can,
to whoever you can.

✫ Get happiness, better health and
self-worth in return.

WE MAKE
A LIVING BY
WHAT WE GET;
WE MAKE A LIFE
BY WHAT
WE GIVE.

Winston Churchill (1874–1965,
UK prime minister and writer, who lived to 90)

STEP 8:
BE POSITIVE

Always look on the bright side of life.
Eric Idle (born 1943, comedian, actor, songwriter)

It's all too easy, with today's attitudes and image of ageing, to believe that getting old is about decrepitude, dependence and dementia. Happily, that negative stereotype is false – as the vast majority of older adults are not physically, cognitively or mentally impaired. Even better, many studies have shown a U-curve of happiness, with those aged 16 to 19 and over 65 being the happiest. For example, in the 2018 UK Office for National Statistics National Well-being programme, a higher proportion of those aged 65 to 84 reported a high level of happiness – nine to ten out of ten! – than all those aged 16 to 64. US data also shows that older people are happier, with around 33 per cent of Americans reporting being very happy at age 88 compared to 24 per cent of those aged 18 to their early twenties.

Nobody loves life like him that's growing old.
Sophocles (c. 497/6–406/5 BCE, Greek playwright)

WHY BE POSITIVE?

If you love life, life will love you back.
Arthur Rubinstein (1887–1982, classical pianist)

There is good evidence that older people whose self-perception of ageing is positive **live on average seven-and-a-half years longer** than those with a negative outlook. Your attitude to life has a significant effect on your health and well-being. For example, a study of 70,000 women showed that optimists had a reduced risk of heart disease, cancer, lung conditions, infection and Type 2 diabetes. And, what's more, if we *believe* we can improve our health, then it really can happen, as the numerous studies using placebos (medicines or treatments with no therapeutic effects, usually used as controls in testing) have demonstrated.

Thinking more positively increases your chances of happiness, motivation, resilience and willingness to participate and enjoy life. Optimism, joy, and a sense of humour are all associated with improved physical and mental health and well-being. And those who are more optimistic are also more likely to be satisfied, even when life is hard.

I'm an optimist – it does not seem to be much use being anything else.
Winston Churchill (1874–1965, UK prime minister and writer)

TIPS

Believe you can and you're halfway there.
Theodore Roosevelt (1858–1919, twenty-sixth US president)

TIP 1

Teach yourself to become more positive and optimistic. It is possible. Only 25 per cent of low optimism is inherited, according to twin studies. So it is largely in your hands. There are many self-help books on the topic and a huge amount of information on the internet – and these tips can also help.

TIP 2

Ignore negative stereotyping about ageing bringing decline, ill health and frailty. First, because it is not true! Over 80 per cent of people over 80, for example, do *not* develop dementia. Second, because research shows that, if you do believe it, you begin to act it out, and then your health and well-being will worsen. And third, it's pointless worrying about ageing – it will happen anyway, if we're lucky!

Age is whatever you think it is. You are as old as you think you are.
Muhammad Ali (1942–2016, boxer, activist and philanthropist)

Old age is one of the most wonderful, sensational,
glorious, fantastic, exciting parts of your whole life.
Charles Eugster (1919–2017, dentist, a world record-
breaking athlete in his nineties, and author at 95)

TIP 3

Seek help if you are depressed or anxious. And don't be embarrassed, ashamed or afraid to talk about it. It can sometimes be extremely hard to cope with all that life may throw at us, without receiving some help. Visit your doctor. There are also many organizations and charities that can assist, including those that deal with mental health, troubled relationships, bereavement or loneliness. Cognitive behavioural therapy (CBT) has proved effective in changing people's thinking and in helping to lift depression. There are practitioners, books and online resources available.

TIP 4

Focus on the positive aspects of getting older and inspiring examples of ageing well. Later life brings many advantages. There are wonderful role models who exemplify how active, happy, healthy and purposeful older people can be, even in the face of adversity. Read about them. And become one yourself. (See **We're Living Longer**, page 11; **Step 6: Be Grateful; It's Never Too Late**, page 148; and **Want to Know More?**, page 157.)

I intend to live forever, or die trying.
Groucho Marx (1890–1977, writer, film star
and comedian, who lived to 87)

TIP 5

Think positively and use positive language. Ban negative self-talk about yourself, your life and the future. Quieten the mind and try to eliminate worrying and judgemental thoughts through meditation or mindfulness. (See Tip 11.) If it works for you, there are many affirmations or "mantras" (a positive phrase that you repeat) that may help. Use inspirational quotes: you can find them on cards, fridge magnets, mugs, prints or in quote books. Or you could write out your favourite uplifting quotes and put them somewhere where you'll see them every day. If you find yourself thinking negatively, challenge yourself. For example, ask what evidence exists for that belief, what is the worst that could happen (it's usually not that bad), and whether the thing that's troubling you will matter in a year's time. Most won't. Changing your thinking and behaviour can be helped by cognitive behavioural therapy (CBT), if it seems to be necessary.

> The happiness of your life depends on
> the quality of your thoughts.
>
> Marcus Aurelius (121–180 CE, Roman emperor, Stoic philosopher)

TIP 6

Accept the things you cannot change, adapt and move forward. We all suffer hardships and bad times. That's life. It's a matter of trying to make the best of it. Try to find something positive in negative circumstances. Believe that however bad things may be (or seem to be), almost all improve, given time. They do. Be patient and compassionate with yourself when going through difficult times. Talk to others, be honest and open, and ask for any help you need.

> **However bad life may seem, there is always something you can do and succeed at. While there's life there's hope.**
> Stephen Hawking (1942–2018, theoretical physicist, cosmologist and author)

> **It's no longer a question of staying healthy. It's a question of finding a sickness you like!**
> Jackie Mason (born 1931, comedian and actor)

TIP 7

Free yourself from bitterness. Don't harbour grudges or compare yourself to others who seem to have more than you, as that only leads to unhappiness and resentment. Focus on yourself instead, and allow yourself to forgive others, and yourself, for past mistakes.

> **Grant me the serenity to accept the things I cannot change, the courage to change the things I can and the wisdom to know the difference.**
> Reinhold Niebuhr (1892–1971, theologian, ethicist and political commentator)

TIP 8

Focus your efforts, time and energy on what you can control and change in your life, for example, the steps in this book that will improve your physical and mental health and your well-being. And, although we cannot always control what happens to us, we can at least control how we react.

> **Everything can be taken from a man but one thing, the last of human freedoms – to choose one's attitude in any given set of circumstances, to choose one's own way.**
> Viktor Frankl (1905–1997, neurologist and psychiatrist, concentration camp survivor)

TIP 9

Be a survivor, not a victim. Avoid a "poor me" victim mentality – which is when a person believes (even in the face of contrary evidence) that they are the victim of fate or the actions of others, and that life is beyond their control and out to hurt them. In these circumstances, help exists, such as cognitive behavioural therapy (CBT). Performing acts of kindness and helping others, practising gratitude and being kinder to yourself can also help you to feel better and more in control of your life. (See **Step 6: Be Grateful** and **Step 7: Give**.)

> Remember you're braver than you believe, stronger than you seem and smarter than you think.
>
> A. A. Milne (1882–1956, author)

TIP 10

Try to eliminate, or at least reduce, harmful stress. A certain amount of stress is good for us, but too much, for too long, causes us to age faster and is bad for our physical and mental health. Positivity and toxic stress are incompatible. Try exercising, eating right, having fun and practising gratitude – they all help to alleviate stress. (See **Step 1: Move**, **Step 2: Eat Right** and **Step 6: Be Grateful**.)

> He who is of calm and happy nature will hardly feel the pressure of age.
>
> Plato (427–347 BCE, Greek philosopher)

TIP 11

Meditate daily. It reduces stress and has additional benefits, such as reducing anxiety, depression and pain, and increasing resilience, relaxation, positive emotions and more. There are courses, groups, books, CDs and apps that teach meditation. Although it takes practice, it is simpler to get started than many imagine and well worth the eventual benefits. Start small, meditating for just three to five minutes a day when you get up. Build up gradually, perhaps up to 20 minutes a day (or more) if you can and if that suits you – everyone is different.

There are various ways to meditate but usually it involves finding somewhere where you will not be distracted. Sit with a straight back and your eyes closed, and focus on your breathing (or less often, a word or object). Count to ten, five breaths in and five breaths out, and then repeat. If your mind wanders, as it will, don't worry, just gently bring it back to your breathing and continue.

> **Where there is peace and meditation there is neither anxiety nor doubt.**
> Saint Francis of Assisi (1181–1226, friar)

TIP 12

Live here and now. Be mindful. The present is the only reality. By living in the moment and focusing completely on what you are doing, you are less likely to worry about the future or ruminate on past regrets. Use all of your senses. For example, for a "mindful meal" concentrate on the taste, texture and aroma of the food and how you feel as you eat; in "mindful walking", walk slowly for, say, five to ten minutes, being aware of your body and breathing, focusing on each step you take and what you can see and hear. Find your "flow" (see **Step 5: Grow**).

TIP 13

Use visualization techniques. They are immensely powerful. Imagine yourself as a joyful, healthy, confident, successful and positive older person. Make it as real as possible: see it, feel it. Do it regularly. Visualization is often used in sport, as well as other areas, to great effect.

> **If you can visualize it, if you can dream it, there's some way to do it.**
> Walt Disney (1901–1966, animator, film producer, entrepreneur and winner of 22 Oscars)

TIP 14

Accept and appreciate imperfection, impermanence and incompleteness – "Wabi-sabi". The long-lived Japanese have the concept of "wabi-sabi" – valuing the beauty of the imperfect, incomplete and transient nature of our world, such as the imperfection of a cracked bowl, the natural cycle of flowers and the falling of leaves. The world, life, your home – and you, too – can be imperfect and incomplete, yet beautiful and valuable. Such a philosophy helps to increase confidence and positivity. So, wrinkles and laughter lines, considered by so many as imperfections to be hidden or removed, in fact have their own beauty and we should embrace them!

> **Beauty is perfect in its imperfections, so you just have to go with the imperfections.**
> Diane von Furstenberg (born 1946, fashion designer)

TIP 15

Associate with positive, happy people, not those who drain your energy and drag you down by constantly bemoaning their lot. Positivity is contagious – ensure you catch it! And once caught, pass it on to others and it will, in the same way, draw others to you and benefit you as well.

> **Those who bring sunshine to the lives of others cannot keep it from themselves.**
> J. M. Barrie (1860–1937, playwright and novelist, creator of Peter Pan)

TIP 16

Believe in yourself and that you, yourself, can make a positive difference to your life and how you age by your actions and thinking. Keep going. Don't give up or give in. (See **Step 5: Grow**.)

> To me, old age is always 15 years older than I am.
> Bernard Baruch (1870–1965, financier, philanthropist and statesman who continued to work until his death at 94)

TIP 17

"Act as if". Changing your behaviour first can actually change the way you think and feel. Act positive even if you don't feel it. If you behave as if you are positive about your life and ageing, you stand a good chance of feeling more positive.

> Act as if you were already happy and that will tend to make you happy.
> Dale Carnegie (1888–1955, writer and speaker on self-improvement)

TIP 18

Do your best: it's enough. Accept who you are. It is difficult to stay positive if you constantly feel you are failing to meet unrealistic, often self-imposed, standards. Aim to be the best you can be and be satisfied with *doing* your best – not necessarily *being* the best. Being "good enough" is good enough.

Life is what you make it, always has been, always will be.
Grandma Moses (1860–1961, famous folk artist who began
painting seriously in her seventies and lived to 101)

The perfect is the enemy of the good.
Voltaire (1694–1778, writer, historian and philosopher)

TIP 19

Frequently do small things that help you to feel more optimistic and positive. For example, wear bright colours or embrace your own unique fashion style; have a massage or aromatherapy treatment; give hugs; watch an inspiring film; read a feel-good book; play; go for a walk in nature; plan pleasurable activities you can look forward to; or even just stand tall with good posture – it makes you feel more optimistic and confident. Be proactive.

A multitude of small delights constitute happiness.
Charles Baudelaire (1821–1867, poet)

TIP 20

Sing, dance and listen to music. Music is "mind medicine". It helps to improve your mood, and reduces stress and depression by releasing one of the brain's "happy chemicals", dopamine. It can even improve cognition skills and memory. And if dancing, you'll be giving yourself some "body medicine" too. Go to a concert or festival – you'll feel uplifted and have the sense of belonging to a like-minded community. (See **"What a Wonderful World" – A Joyful Playlist**, page 154).

> **Without music life would be a mistake.**
> Friedrich Nietzsche (1844–1900, philosopher)

TIP 21

Laugh. Find things to do that make you laugh more. Laughter stimulates the release of endorphins (another of those "happy chemicals") and puts you in a positive mood. It can also reduce stress, pain, depression and anxiety, boost your immune system, and improve your sleep quality and memory. Laugh at yourself. Listen to or watch comedy shows or stand-up comedy on radio, television or YouTube. Read a funny book. We laugh more when interacting with others, so socialize – perhaps go out to a comedy act or film.

> **Always laugh when you can. It is cheap medicine.**
> Lord Byron (1788–1824, poet)

TIP 22

And finally, follow the other seven steps in this book. They will all contribute to your feeling happier, more positive, and more engaged in life.

> **Happiness depends upon ourselves.**
> Aristotle (384–322 BCE, Greek philosopher)

IN SUMMARY:

✧ You can learn to think, feel and be positive.

✧ Better health, happiness and
a longer life will follow.

THE MORE YOU PRAISE AND CELEBRATE LIFE, THE MORE THERE IS IN LIFE TO CELEBRATE.

Oprah Winfrey (born 1954, media
executive, talk show host, actress
and philanthropist)

IT'S NEVER TOO LATE

**Go confidently in the direction of your dreams.
Live the life you've imagined.**
Henry David Thoreau (1817–1862, essayist, poet,
philosopher and naturalist)

There are countless people who do wonderful things in later life, most of whom are unknown outside the circle of their colleagues, family and friends.

But here are some famous people, aged 50 to 100 years old, who show us that you are never too old, and it is never too late, to do something new, be of value or achieve greatness.

Age is a number. It's something imposed on you.
Dame Judi Dench (born 1934, actress)

IN THEIR FIFTIES:

Charles Darwin (1809–1882) published *On the Origin of Species* at 50 (1859).

Leonardo da Vinci (1452–1519) painted the *Mona Lisa* at 51 (1503–1506).

George Frideric Handel (1685–1759) conducted the first performance of his *Messiah* at 57 (1742).

Alexandre Gustave Eiffel (1832–1923) completed the Eiffel Tower at 57 (1889).

Daniel Defoe's (1660–1731) first novel *Robinson Crusoe* was published when he was 59 (1719).

IN THEIR SIXTIES:

Lise Meitner (1878–1968) became the first person to describe nuclear fission at 60 (1938).

Dame Margot Fonteyn (1919–1991) danced at the Royal Ballet until she was 61 (1980).

Charles Flint (1850–1934) founded IBM at 61.

Louis Pasteur (1822–1895) gave the first injection against rabies at 62 (1885).

James Parkinson (1755–1824) identified Parkinson's disease at 62 (1817).

J. R. R. Tolkien (1892–1973) was 62 when *The Lord of the Rings* was published (1954–1955).

Sir Winston Churchill (1874–1965) first became prime minister at 65 (1940) and again at age 76 (1951).

Sir Ranulph Fiennes (born 1944) climbed Everest at 65 (2009).

Ronald Reagan (1911–2004) became US president at 69 (1981).

IN THEIR SEVENTIES:

Golda Meir (1898–1978) became prime minister of Israel at 70 (1969).

Elton John (born 1947) is still entertaining us having passed the age of 70.

Brenda Hale (born 1945) became president of the UK Supreme Court at 72 (2017).

Joanna Lumley (born 1946) is still working as an actress and activist in her seventies.

Bob Hope (1903–2003) was still working at 75.

Nelson Mandela (1918–2013) was elected president of South Africa at 75 (1994).

Michelangelo (1475–1564) was the architect of St Peter's Basilica in his seventies.

The Rolling Stones (born between 1936 and 1943) are still rocking and rolling in their seventies.

Pope Francis (born 1936) became the 266th pope in 2013, at the age of 76.

John Glenn (1921–2016) is the oldest man to have travelled in space, in the *Discovery* space shuttle, aged 77 (1998).

Phil Knight (born 1938), co-founder of Nike, was CEO until the age of 78, when he became chairman emeritus.

Giuseppe Verdi (1813–1901) wrote his opera *Othello* in his seventies and *Falstaff* aged 80 (1893).

IN THEIR EIGHTIES:

Dames Maggie Smith and Judi Dench (both born in 1934), and Dame Joan Collins (born 1933) continue acting in their eighties.

David Hockney, OM (born 1937), is still working as an artist, and made his first stained-glass window (for Westminster Abbey) at 81 (2018).

Joan Rivers (1933–2014) was still working as a comedian and author up to her death at 81.

Sir Laurence Olivier (1907–1989) continued acting, despite ill health, until his death at 82.

Fred Astaire (1899–1987) died aged 88 after a film and television career spanning 76 years.

Claude Monet (1840–1926) continued painting in his eighties.

Warren Buffett (born 1930), one of the world's richest men, CEO and chairman, is still working, and a notable philanthropist in his eighties.

Lord Denning (1899–1999), Master of the Rolls and Law Lord, retired after 38 years as a judge, at age 83.

Coco Chanel (1883–1971) still ran her fashion empire at 85.

Ruth Bader Ginsburg (born 1933) is still active in the US Supreme Court in her eighties.

Dr Charles Eugster (1919–2017) took up bodybuilding at 87 and sprinting at 95, becoming a world record-holding athlete.

IN THEIR NINETIES – AND HUNDREDS:

Pablo Picasso (1881–1973) was still working as an artist at 90.

Oliver Wendell Holmes (1841–1935) and John Paul Stevens (born 1920) both served on the US Supreme Court until they were 90 years old.

Sir David Attenborough (born 1926) is still travelling the world making natural history documentaries in his nineties.

Frank Lloyd Wright (1867–1959) was working on his Guggenheim Museum at his death, aged 91.

Mel Brooks (born 1926) filmmaker, actor, comedian and author is still working in his nineties.

Eli Wallach (1915–2014) was still acting in the year of his death aged 98.

Elizabeth II (born 1926), in her nineties, has been Queen of the UK, Canada, Australia and New Zealand since 1952.

Fauja Singh (born 1911) ran his first marathon at 89 and was running marathons at 100.

Dame Vera Lynn (born 1917), when aged 100, released an album that reached number 3 in the UK album charts.

IF WE DID ALL THE THINGS WE ARE CAPABLE OF, WE WOULD LITERALLY ASTOUND OURSELVES.

Thomas Edison (1847–1931, prolific inventor, who died aged 84)

"WHAT A WONDERFUL WORLD" — A JOYFUL PLAYLIST

I have pulled together 21 inspiring and joyful songs. Many have videos on YouTube.

It is a personal choice, and could have been much longer!

Music can be incredibly powerful in transforming emotions, and this playlist is guaranteed to put a smile on my face, make me get up and dance, feel stronger and more positive, or simply feel hugely grateful for my loved ones, life and our beautiful world.

You may find a few in this selection that are new to you. I hope you like them.

Please listen and enjoy!

1.   "What a Wonderful World" – Louis Armstrong
2.   "Don't Stop Me Now" – Queen
3.   "Bring Me Sunshine" – Morecambe and Wise
4.   "We are the World" – USA for Africa
5.   "I'm Still Standing" – Elton John
6.   "Smile" – Nat King Cole
7.   "Dancing Queen" – Abba
8.   "It's My Life" – Bon Jovi
9.   "Wind Beneath My Wings" – Bette Midler
10. "Don't Rain on My Parade" – Barbra Streisand
11. "I am Somebody" – Santana/WILL.I.AM
12. "Happy" – Pharrell Williams
13. "To Life" – Chaim Topol
14. "I Am What I Am" – Shirley Bassey
15. "Get Happy" – Judy Garland
16. "The Best" – Tina Turner
17. "Pick Yourself Up" – Fred Astaire
18. "I Will Survive" – Gloria Gaynor
19. "Always Look on the Bright Side of Life" – Monty Python
20. "Ain't Got No, I Got Life" – Nina Simone
21. "We Have All the Time in the World" – Louis Armstrong

AND TOMORROW?

Ageing is an extraordinary process where you become the person you always should have been.

David Bowie (1947–2016, singer and songwriter)

Who knows what future years may bring? I'm only in my late sixties and there's still so much I want to discover and do. With these eight steps, a lot of dancing, a little luck, and hopefully a few good genes (my mother just missed her 100th birthday), I'm planning to be around enjoying what life has to offer for several decades yet.

Confucius (551–479 BCE), the Chinese philosopher and teacher, said: **"Old age, believe me, is a good and pleasant thing."** I will embrace old age eventually, but prefer the philosophy of George Burns, the comedian who lived and worked to 100. He advised: **"You can't help getting older, but you don't have to get old."**

I hope you, too, get a whole lot older and more joyful.

WANT TO KNOW MORE?

Here follows a short, personal selection of books, reports and websites, for more information, references and sources, both serious and amusing. The list is very far from comprehensive but many of those listed contain detailed research references and further reading.

And remember, it's worth following some Twitter accounts on healthy ageing – including mine: *Age Joyfully @AgeingBetter*.

Books: advice and guidance

The 100-Year Life – Lynda Gratton and Andrew Scott (2016) Bloomsbury
Age is Just a Number – Charles Eugster (2017) Sphere
Aging Well – George E. Vaillant (2002) Little, Brown & Company
Bolder: Making the Most of Our Longer Lives – Carl Honoré (2018) Simon & Schuster
Disrupt Aging – Jo Ann Jenkins (2016) Public Affairs
Growing Old – Des Wilson (2014) Quartet
How to Age – Anne Karpf (2014) Macmillan
How to Age Positively – Guy Robertson (2014) Positive Ageing Associates
How to Live Forever: The Enduring Power of Connecting the Generations – Marc Freedman (2018) Public Affairs
Ikigai: The Japanese Secret to a Long and Happy Life – Hector Garcia and Francesc Miralles (2017) Penguin Random House
Iris Apfel: Accidental Icon – Iris Apfel (2018) Harper Design

The Nordic Guide to Living Longer – Bertil Marklund (2017) Piatkus
The Second Half of Your Life – Jill Shaw Ruddock (2011) Vermilion, Ebury
A Short Guide to a Long Life – David Agus (2014) Simon & Schuster
Sod 60! –Claire Parker and Muir Gray (2016)
Sod 70! –Muir Gray (2015) Bloomsbury

Fun books (quotes, illustrations, etc.)

Older, Wiser, Sexier – Bev Williams (2010) Summersdale
Wrinklies' Wit & Wisdom: Humorous Quotes About Getting On A Bit – Rosemarie Jarski (2005) Prion
You're Not Old You're Vintage – Sarah Viner (2014) Summersdale
You're Only Young Twice – Quentin Blake (2008) Andersen Press

Reports and research references, etc.

Doing Good? Altruism and Wellbeing in an Age of Austerity, Mental Health Foundation (2012)
Index of Wellbeing in Later Life, Age UK Policy & Research Department (February 2017)
Later Life in 2015, Centre for Ageing Better (2015)
Measuring National Well-being: At What Age is Personal Well-being the Highest?, UK Office of National Statistics (February 2016)
Measuring National Well-being: Quality of Life in the UK, Office of National Statistics (2018)
The Perennials: the Future of Ageing, Ipsos Mori Report (13 February 2019)
The Power of Purposeful Aging: Culture Change and the New Demography, Milken Institute Center for the Future of Aging (December 2016)

Start Active, Stay Active: Report on Physical Activity in the UK, Department of Health, four UK Chief Medical Officers (updated in 2016)

If You're Feeling Lonely. How to Stay Connected in Older Age, Independent Age (November 2016)

Some useful websites

(Most are also on social media, such as Twitter and Facebook)

www.aarpinternational.org (American Non-Profit for those 50 and older)

www.ageactionalliance.org

www.ageing-better.org.uk (Centre For Ageing Better)

www.ageofnoretirement.org

www.ageuk.org.uk

www.carersuk.org

www.contact-the-elderly.org.uk

www.do-it.org (volunteering)

www.gov.uk/phe (Public Health England)

www.ilcuk.org.uk (International Longevity Centre)

www.independentage.org

www.ncvo.org.uk (volunteering)

www.nhs.uk

www.openage.org.uk (a successful community model for ageing well)

www.positiveageingassociates.com

www.un.org/development/desa/ageing (UN Focal Point on Ageing)

www.u3a.org.uk (University of the Third Age)

www.volunteeringmatters.org.uk

www.who.int (World Health Organization on ageing and life-course)

If you're interested in finding out more about our books, find us on Facebook at **Summersdale Publishers** and follow us on Twitter at **@Summersdale.**

www.summersdale.com